To Dave,

One of my greatest thrills as a broadcaster was working with you. You are a PRO!

Mark
Cha

THE COACH AND THE GEEK

Building a Kick-Butt Culture

Mark Adams and Jeff Van Fleet

Forward by

Mark A. Parrish

Printed in the United States of America

First Printing, February 2020
Minor Revision, April 2020

ISBN 978-1-64764-996-8

Cover art by Joseph Studios
www.josephstudios.net

Foreword by Mark Parrish
www.parrishpartners.com

Dedications

This book is dedicated to all of my players who carried me to two championships and a small college hall of fame coaching career.

Mark Adams

I dedicate this book

to my parents, Pete and Anna, for their support and encouragement through my formative years, for teaching me the value of hard work, and for teaching me that everyone should be valued and respected.

to my incredibly talented, beautiful, smart, and insightful daughters, Catie and Rachel. Thank you for your never-ending support, and for your thoughtful and heartfelt words and uplifting presence.

to my smart, beautiful, strong, and sassy wife and partner, Sandy. You make me a better person. You challenge me to think differently and see things from other perspectives. You remind all of us to choose kindness. I appreciate you for these things, and for your years of unwavering encouragement and strength in supporting me.

Jeff Van Fleet

Table of Contents

iv / THE COACH AND THE GEEK

Foreword

Over more than thirty years, my professional journey has taken me from battlefield to boardroom and from cockpit to corporate. Throughout I have served as a serial CEO in the public, private and private equity sectors. In each subsequent engagement, I have rigorously sought to recreate the culture of commitment I enjoyed earlier in my career as a commissioned officer and AH-64 Apache helicopter pilot in the U.S. Army.

As part of my very personal journey of continuous improvement, I've remained a lifelong learner and student practitioner of principle-centered leadership. Principle-centered leadership provides the foundation upon which execution excellence is built. In building a culture committed to continuous improvement, one destined for excellence, those at the helm of the organization must consider self-mastery—the ability to lead oneself—as vital to leading others competently.

I've heard it said, "Humans can live three weeks without food, three days without water and three minutes without air, but not one second longer without hope." In *THE COACH AND THE GEEK, Building a Kick-Butt Culture*, Adams and Van Fleet offer a hope-filled tutorial on principle-centered leadership through an entertaining, inspiring and always fun to read sports novelette. These entrepreneurs and seasoned business leaders codify practical, everyday principles of self-mastery that help the protagonist overcome the despair of personal struggles, professional failures and a life devoid of hope. In their work, they capture time tested methods to bounce back from seemingly insurmountable odds with discipline and delight.

Each chapter introduces self-mastery principles for leaders in all stages of development. Whether currently a CEO, a department head, a company founder or a budding entrepreneur, this work is intended as an aid for aspiring leaders at every level of development aiming to produce daily their career best effort.

Like me, I suspect you will find hope within its pages.

Mark A. Parrish

Managing Partner of Parrish Partners, President & CEO (former) of Igloo Products Corp, President & CEO (former) of Stuart Dean Company, Inc., Graduate of the United States Military Academy, West Point and former US Army Captain

Chapter One: Losing sucks

Coach Woodward sat alone in his rented, small two-bedroom house. It was quiet, very quiet. It's the kind of quiet a loser knows after the final buzzer of a twenty-point loss at home. He sat there and stared at the boring green walls. He was empty. He was hopeless. He was devoid of any answers as to how to fix his team.

He rose, turned on the burner and retrieved a skillet. It was 11:03 PM and all he could think to do was make pancakes. Don't ask why. After a lopsided, 22-point loss at home, nothing makes sense. Why not pancakes? He flipped over one, then another, and another until all the pancake mix was gone. Eighteen pancakes in all stacked like Pisa. He ate as many as he could. Don't ask why.

Scott Woodward is a young coach and a rising star in college basketball, at least until he took the job at Bozeman Tech. His team was 3-25 his first season and slightly better at 8-20 the next. That was their 17th consecutive losing season and Coach Woodward owned two of those losing seasons. Now his third team was 0-3 and the future prospect of his program looked bleak. The team played as if devoid of hope and there were no easy wins in sight.

Coach Woodward was in between sleep and awake after a belly full of pancakes. He laid in bed, a restless limbo that typified his current existence. He was going nowhere, his team was a nightmare, his future in doubt.

Woodward is a basketball coach who now questions his own abilities. He is stuck on his own leadership island. He is retreating to his own despair. What now?

Lesson 1

 We all face failure. The initial reaction we have to failure is typically to feel sorry for ourselves. It is how we deal with the failure that defines us.

Chapter Two: ME versus WE

Coach Woodward woke up to a busy Friday morning schedule. First was a staff meeting, then a sit-down with his athletic director, then a noon luncheon to speak to a bunch of upset boosters and local business leaders. After all that, he had a video session with the team, practice, then was off to watch a local high school kid play.

When you win, this schedule is fun. When you lose, it feels like total despair. Woodward couldn't shake the previous night's loss and everyone he saw had some words of encouragement. "Tough one coach." "Get it Saturday." "The sun came up Coach. It's a new day. Get the next one." What a pain to have all these "well-intentioned fans" remind him of how much he and the team stunk the night before. While all were pleasant and nice to his face, he knew most were plotting to get him fired.

The staff meeting was the same old crap just a different day. Coaches complained about not enough support, lack of execution, and players who were not committed. Coach Woodward listened but soon tuned everyone out. It was all his fault and he knew it.

Then came the meeting with his boss.

Alan Johnson was the athletic director and to say that he and Coach Woodward didn't get along would be a massive understatement. Years ago, Alan had applied for the job as head coach but never got it. Now, he was the athletic director through tenure and luck, and he thought he had all the answers. To make matters worse, Alan did not hire Coach Woodward and he seemed keen on trying to get his own guy on board. At least those were the rumors around town.

As Woodward entered Johnson's office, his boss didn't even raise his eyes or say hello. Instead, Woodward was greeted with a terse, "Sit down, Scott."

"You only drew 2,132 fans last night and you got your butt whipped!" he snapped. Coach Woodward was used to the "You not We" direction of these conversations. Next would be the "I" version of the discussion.

Right on cue Johnson said, "I am tired of watching your team lose. I am tired of being embarrassed. I am sick of watching you coach a team that doesn't play the way the teams played when I coached." Johnson's tone was condescending and stated every "I" with an extra emphasis. Woodward sat and stared at his boss in silence for a few seconds.

"Is that it, Alan?" Coach Woodward asked sarcastically. They stared at each other.

Coach Woodward thought, what a self-absorbed jerk his boss was. Woodward wanted to build a culture of WE. He believed in a selfless culture. He wanted his team to be based on sacrificing for the good of all team members. Unfortunately, he had a boss who continued to waste away from the 'Disease of Me!' Alan was self-absorbed and constantly spoke in terms of "I" not "we." Alan's top priority was Alan himself.

Woodward got up to walk out.

Johnson yelled, "Sit down! I'm not done!" Woodward didn't skip a step as he opened the door and left his boss in his angry wake.

Woodward had no more time for distractions from his boss. He had to prepare for practice.

Lesson 2

 The 'Disease of Me' is a selfish virus that destroys organizations. One person with this disease, regardless of position within your organization can spread the contagion and influence your entire team if left unchecked. As a leader, look for signs of this virus. Look for people who constantly look outward to place blame. People who focus on themselves and use the words, "I" and "me" are potential carriers. Look for these warning signs.

Chapter Three: Stop blaming everyone else!!

Coach Woodward met with his staff before practice. His assistant coaches sensed his frustration as they watched the video of the previous night's game. Woodward squirmed in his chair, sighed in exasperation, and complained out loud, "We just worked on that two days ago!" as he watched a lay-up by an opposing player.

Assistant coaches began to chime in to support what they thought was their boss's narrative. It was a coaching feeding frenzy, blaming the players while taking no responsibility for their own contribution to the lack of execution.

Woodward had seen and heard enough. He exploded, "SHUT UP!"

Every coach saw the anger on Woodward's red face, combined with eyes glaring like a rabid dog. There was total and uncomfortable silence.

Woodward barked for everyone to leave his office. Each assistant coach slunk out wanting to disappear, and not be noticed as an accomplice to the lack of execution of their team. Every coach knew why Coach Woodward was so upset. While they all wanted to place blame on the players, Woodward blamed himself, and his silence was an indictment on his coaching staff's lack of self-awareness.

Lesson 3

 The 'Disease of Me' starts often with well-intentioned and even hard-working people who experience failure and then look away from their own mirror. It is always easier to blame someone else. Every organization needs someone to challenge that behavior immediately or the dysfunction can grow ... and grow quickly.

Chapter Four: One great question can lead to answers, a lot of answers

Coach Woodward had been divorced for two years. His marriage was short, only three years, and didn't last because of many reasons, the least of which was a lack of balance in his own life. He was also the product of an alcoholic family and those experiences had long-term repercussions. He internalized those early life demons, and while he was always eager to please and be a good and loyal friend, he was not a good and loyal husband. It finally caught up to him. Now he was married to basketball.

Today, that marriage to this game was again torturing his life. The challenge coaches face is not whether they win or lose but instead how they can handle winning and losing. Dealing with a win is easy. A winning coach goes out with friends at a local pub or someone's home and celebrates the win. You are the hometown hero.

Losing is a whole different animal. Losing can devour a coach! They stink and they know it – and so does everyone else.

After the coaches meeting earlier that afternoon, Scott went home, grabbed a beer, and started watching game video. It was his routine. There is comfort in repetition. As he watched the video, some new ideas started to creep into his mind. He might have even said he moved a bit from feeling like a total failure to being a tiny bit hopeful. "Maybe we can figure something out," he said to himself. Coach Woodward wrote down some notes to share with his staff. While this loss stung, he was beginning to develop a new path forward. The coach finally fell asleep and slept soundly.

Coach Woodward woke up energized. While video study was tedious and sometimes maddening, it was also instructive. And last night he learned a lot. The good news was that he realized he had a team that could sustain significant effort and execution for short periods of time, but not well enough to win games. Woodward still felt that energy as he drove to his office and headed for work. Coach Woodward saw some excellent execution in the video last night from his team individually and collectively in spurts, but they were only able to sustain their effort for a few minutes at a time. Interestingly, these spurts of stellar execution were sometimes rebounding, other times it was ball movement, and the rest of the time it was defensive hustle.

How could he create consistency? How could he best teach the most important behaviors of a winning team without focusing solely on wins and losses? Woodward knew he needed his assistants and players more engaged. Could he find a way that would motivate the team and help them gain confidence in themselves and each other?

As he pulled onto campus and began walking to his office, something his dad taught him years ago came into his head. Whenever he and his brothers would get into trouble, instead of yelling at them, his dad would first ask them what they could have done differently.

Coach got to his office, took off his gloves and coat, and walked down the quiet hallway to grab a coffee, black as he needed a jolt. As he got back to his desk, he was still thinking about those times with his dad. He pulled out his notes from the night before and a thought occurred to him as his assistant coaches began coming into his office. Instead of the usual banter, it felt tense. They were all hoping for a better meeting than the previous day's explosive blame-fest. Scott looked each assistant in the eye and then said, "Listen guys, we have to do better. And I don't mean on the court. I mean that we need to do better. We are all better than this. You are better than this." He hesitated, "And, I am better than this too. No more blaming each other or the kids. We need to do something differently."

Scott paused as he once again looked into the eyes of his coaches, and asked in a calm voice, "If you could only ask me one question today, what would your question be?"

He nodded to his associate head coach, Porter "Jake" Jacobsen. Jake thought about the question for a few seconds and asked, "Coach, how can we get better?" Woodward nodded but gave no response.

Next was assistant coach Donnie Matta, "Do we have good enough talent to win our league championship?" Woodward nodded but again, no response was given.

Assistant coach Kevin Holly was next, "Are we playing hard enough?" Woodward nodded once more.

Then it was time for the youngest coach in the meeting to ask his one question. Coach Jason White was an up and coming graduate assistant coach and was the technology geek on the staff. He was on point to evaluate and edit video for all team video sessions. He was young, enthusiastic, innovative, and perceptive beyond his years.

Jason took a deep breath and looked Woodward in the eye, "Coach Woodward, with all due respect, our team is not great at anything. Why? Because we as coaches have not defined what greatness means for our team. As a starting point, I want to ask you, what do you want our team to be great at?"

Coach Jacobsen, the head coach's right-hand man looked at Jason and said, "Holy crap, now that's a great question!"

Woodward was taken aback by the simplicity of that question but also by its power. He started talking to himself out loud, "What do we want to be great at? Hmmm." Then, thoughts started flowing to him. "We're kind of good in many areas, but not great at anything. We can't be consistent unless we are great at something, and we can't get great unless we first decide what we want to be great at as a team. What a helluva question!" Woodward concluded.

Woodward smiled as he knew positive change was about to take flight. The room was kind of buzzing. With one simple question a new culture was being born! The youngest member of the coaching staff just earned everyone's respect by sharing one question that could change the course of the season.

Coach Woodward leaned back in his chair and then quickly leaned forward, half standing up with both hands' fingertips on top of the desk as if ready to pounce like a mountain lion on a big horn sheep. He was hungry for long-term success, not just a win.

"OK. What style of play do I love? Intense! Tough! I want our team to play hard and have fun! I want us to be a great defensive team! I want to create chaos for the opposing team. I want to defensively dominate the conference. I'm tired of losing and that losing stops right now," Woodward concluded as he slapped his hand on the desk.

"Jason, you are on point. You have 48 hours to report back to me with a plan to be a great defensive team. I want a new approach. Leverage anyone you know for ideas. I'm open to anything -- I want us to become a great defensive team." Woodward continued. "Be as innovative as you like. There are no boundaries. There are no bad ideas. Any questions?"

"No, sir," Jason said as he now became the coach in the room with the most responsibility at 25 years of age.

Jason left the room and got goose bumps. One great question led him down a path to answers he didn't know just yet. But those answers would come. He knew it! This was his chance. Now what?

Lesson 4

 Jason first asked a 'WHY' question then followed up with a 'What' question. 'Why' is the key question in any effort when developing a plan. Anyone can ask a 'What' question. 'Why' requires more thought and can provide greater depth while identifying the real challenge.

Chapter Five: Introducing the Geek

Ron Marshall had a decision to make, blue jeans or khakis? He chose blue jeans.

Marshall drove to work for another day at Leola Data Systems. Marshall had a wife, one little dude, and until recently, a seemingly bright future.

He entered the office building, swiped his security badge, and walked among the sea of cubicles passing one after another. It was quiet, except for muffled clicks of the keyboards and an occasional sigh of exasperation. A few whispers cascaded over the IT geometry of workstations. Some whispered suggestions to colleagues, others whispered their weekend plans, others looked at Marshall as he quickly walked past them without a word. They waited for him to pass and then complained in hushed tones.

Ron was oblivious to it all. His software project was way over budget, woefully beyond any reasonable deadline, and had so many bugs that Raid would be overwhelmed.

RON MARSHALL, DIRECTOR OF IT was the door sign which greeted him every morning as he entered his cluttered and disheveled office. This surely would be another day of hair loss. Long, pointless meetings dotted his calendar with more tail-chasing and blame-game executives who would be sure to put that blame all on him. He was beyond frustrated and his future was in doubt.

Ron Marshall closed the door behind him and turned on his computer. His goal was to dive into his screen and not be noticed. His office was at the end of the hallway, the perfect place to hide.

Ron Marshall is an IT leader who now questions his own abilities. He is stuck on his own leadership island. He is retreating to his own despair. What now?

Lesson 5

 Leaders often feel trapped on their own island. The more you isolate yourself the more desolate that island becomes.

Chapter Six: Truth hurts

Ron quickly checked his emails. Only 200 emails since closing time yesterday. How in the heck can you get 200 emails overnight? The answer is simple, India. The country never sleeps. He was overwhelmed again, and the day had just begun with his outsourced partner in India sending plenty of bad news and plenty of re-work for his US-based team to review and correct.

Leola Data Systems has an "open-door policy", but doors were often closed, especially when multiple projects were taking twice as much time as projected and costing twice as much money. And those were the good projects! Ron had learned over time that deadlines were merely a suggestion. Excuses were commonplace as finger pointing was always the norm.

The CIO hated the CFO, who really hated the CMO, and all of them hated the CEO who was a sales guy by trade. The organization was a mess and blame, easy to assign. Accountability was lost in the confusing data-driven abyss, which provided a safe haven for the 'cover your ass' crowd.

Everyone wanted more money for their department. Everyone wanted more electronic toys to sell to enhance the customer experience, but none were willing to ask the customer what they really wanted or needed. Everyone wanted credit when things went well. No one accepted responsibility when projects went south, lost $3M and crashed their system. With this "culture" and management's egos, nobody was encouraged to peel back the covers and look at the core problems. If someone tried – and Ron tried in his first couple of years – they were called a "smokestack" and were told to focus on their department and quit looking for stuff to fix. Ron remembers thinking, *how the heck can we get better if we're never allowed to talk about the problems?*

Oh well. That was a long time ago, and now, Ron Marshall hated his job. He hated the political CYA mentality. He hated the top-down driven culture. Most of all, he hated that he had become one of them. He was about to show everyone just how much he hated his job.

The weekly status meeting that was about to start would surely be a disaster. The leadership team decided to join the meeting and Ron would be presenting a status update on the Win-To-Fin (WTF) Project. Never did an acronym fit so well for a Windows integration to a financial tool software project. This gave him a bit of secretive pleasure.

Ron opened the meeting with an update that the development team was behind schedule. He explained that the business had changed requirements and now the dev team was in reaction mode. Immediately, the VP of sales and marketing, Vance Palm, went on the attack.

"Our customers are clamoring for this new edition. Why is it taking so long?" Palm asked.

Ron took a deep breath, "This project was planned but we could never get the stakeholders attention long enough to figure out what they really wanted, and we had to get started. There has been constant change. Every time we finish some functionality and think we have a clear path forward someone new from your team gets involved and changes their mind about what we already built. All of these new demands constantly change our team's direction and creates a bunch of churn!"

Palm leaned forward and pointed his finger, "So it's our fault you can't keep your promises? Maybe, just maybe it's your fault for not managing the project properly. Every time we ask for a date, that date passes and all we do is make excuses to our customers. We promised WTF six months ago. WTF?"

While some laughed, others recoiled. Ron knew there was some truth to what Palm was saying, but it wasn't all his team's fault. He pulled up a slide that documented all the changes others had thrown their way along with the impact in time, money, and extra effort his department absorbed. He explained that their process was flawed and too reactive. All the business' stakeholders felt like they could walk over to their favorite developer and ask them to prioritize their pet feature over all others. It created a chaotic mess!

"As a management team, aren't you concerned about the ad hoc nature of our internal processes?" Ron asked. "You can blame us but maybe you should look in the damn mirror!"

A sudden hush fell over the room. Ron had just challenged the entire leadership team. Every director made a concerted effort not to make eye contact with anyone in that room. Ron sat down and he could feel the eyes staring a hole in him from all directions. Then he looked at the CIO who mouthed, "SEE ME."

About an hour later Ron met with his boss. It wasn't a long meeting. Five minutes later, Ron was packing up his belongings in a cardboard box and heading home to find a new job. WTF!

Lesson 6

 As real coaches, we often face the challenge of dealing with self-centered CYA managers. Teams will surely lose with selfish ego-centric leadership.

Chapter Seven: Sometimes opportunity comes wrapped in strange packages

As Ron Marshall drove home on that fateful day, he was discouraged and frustrated and frankly, pissed off. He didn't deserve this. He had worked his butt off, well, at least for a while. Then the "system" got to him and he began acting like the rest of them. "Damn it! I just got fired!" he said out loud.

Now, he was upset with himself and shame came slipping in. "I became part of the problem, too."

However, the long drive home started to clear his head a little and a thought from a long time ago came creeping back in. It was a saying by his high school basketball coach, and it kept rotating through his thoughts, *sometimes opportunity comes wrapped in strange packages.*

Ron's high school coach taught him that philosophy on the day he was demoted as a starter on the Saint Benedict High School team in 1995. That was a hard day, but over time, it turned out to be a good one. Ron learned how to compete that day, how to fill a role, and how to help his team win. He accepted the challenge of his new role as the 6th man, and he began to embody the team motto: *Every day in every way, we get a little better.*

Ron also learned that hard work doesn't always get rewarded, but focused work for the good of the team was usually rewarded in positive team results. Not only did his high school team win their district championship, but Ron also dedicated himself to better academic performance and eventually earned an academic scholarship to Bozeman Tech. In every way, Ron got better!

"How did I forget all those lessons about teamwork?" Ron reflected on his way home. He was upset, but not with his boss, or his development team, or his company. He was upset with himself. He became a blame agent just like everyone else at the precise time when he could have set the right example.

Why didn't he take the blame, or take the time to develop some well-thought out solutions, and why didn't he support and protect his team like he did in high school? Ron thought to himself, *Damn it.*

This was a tough day and a very hard lesson learned but as he drove, he came back to *Sometimes opportunity comes wrapped in strange packages.*

Lesson 7

 If/when you lose your job, take some time to mourn, but only a short time (no more than 5 days, but ideally only 24 hours), then start plotting a path forward. Opportunity truly does come wrapped in strange packages!

Chapter Eight: The puker!

Ron Marshall arrived home at 1:30 PM. His wife, Ellen, worked at the local gift shop and she wouldn't be home until 4 o'clock. His little dude, Freddy, was at pre-school. Freddy was high energy. The kind of high energy that drove some adults crazy, but Ron loved watching him discover new things.

Last night Ron took Freddy to a Bozeman Tech basketball game and they sat in the front row. Ron is an accommodating parent, especially when it's just him and Freddy, at least that's what he calls himself. Others might call him something like an over-accommodating father raising a little hellion.

Freddy wanted popcorn, so he got popcorn. Freddy wanted a Coke, so he got a Coke. Freddy wanted a hot dog, so he got a hot dog. Freddy wanted cotton candy, so he got cotton candy. Then in the 4th quarter, Freddy projectile vomited on the court just as the home team was getting blown out in the final minute.

The referees called a time-out so the floor could be cleaned. Student workers descended on the eclectic mix of liquid color on the floor. Some of them handled it better than others, but one of those students hurled his own liquid onto the court before they eventually got it all cleaned up.

"Oh my god!" Coach Scott Woodward uttered barely audible and to no one in particular. "That pretty much sums it up!"

Mercifully, the final buzzer sounded, and dad and son exited the building as quickly as possible. Freddy asked for candy on the way out. Ron didn't say a word, he just wanted to get out of there, humiliated and horrified by what had just happened. Coach Woodward felt the exact same way but for different reasons.

Lesson 8

 Ron is a loving and supportive father. Maybe too loving and supportive but still, a good father. This new Dad learned a valuable lesson on this night. Four-year-old children should never make their own food choices 😊

Chapter Nine: Get your butt out of bed!

Ellen didn't make much money at the gift shop, but she loved the work and it helped provide a few extras for the family. She paid the family bills and balanced the checkbook and sometimes when the Marshall's got in a tight bind, she had to get creative with credit cards. She knew a lot more about their finances than Ron. Ellen grew up in a poor section of town, the kind of place where cars were up on blocks and people collected old TVs -- in their yards. Ron appreciated her attention to detail and due diligence with their family finances, but it also created some friction on occasion.

Ron now sat alone at home knowing Ellen would not react well to the news that he was now unemployed. Heck, he didn't even know how much money was in their savings account, but Ron did have a bit of a silver lining to his bad news.

Ron had started at Leola Data Systems over 20 years ago, right out of college, and his severance package was generous. Because of his longevity with the company, he had accrued one month of pay for every two years of service, capped at six months. Plus, he had accrued a month's worth of vacation time that would be cashed out to him. This gave him seven months' worth of severance money to find a new job.

Ron knew he needed to develop a short-term plan for Ellen to settle her concerns. He thought about a Mr. Mom role to save daycare expenses. That might make her feel better. Then he thought about his four-year-old's projectile vomit spewing on the court from the previous night. He decided maybe he wasn't the next Michael Keaton.

Ron needed a change. He needed a plan to restart his career. It certainly paid the bills nicely and made for a consistent income, but was he really happy? "Heck NO!" he said out loud.

However, Ron needed to face facts as he had just lost his job. His project was a failure. He needed to take ownership in his own failure. It was time to accept responsibility, stop blaming others and begin to rebuild. He muttered, "Pick yourself up, loser."

Just then Ellen walked through the door. "Who are you talking to? Who is a loser?"

"Me," Ron said with a sheepish grin and a look away nod.

Ellen asked quizzically, "Why are you home so early?" Ron asked her to sit down. He recounted his day and the longer he talked, the more Ellen became a human ball of yarn. She curled up with knees to her chin and arms wrapped around her legs. It was a defense mechanism Ron was all too familiar with. He could see in her eyes that she was already living out of a beat-up family truckster while sleeping underneath an overpass on I-90 at night. Given Ellen's upbringing, it was easy for her to see this snowballing. In her mind she was not only broke, but also homeless and probably pregnant with quintuplets.

Ron stopped after detailing the meeting with his boss. Ellen closed her eyes, took a deep breath and then tears started rolling down her cheeks.

He went over, put his arms around her and just held her. After a few minutes, Ellen stopped crying, and unraveled herself, and started to accept their new reality. As they sat together, she began transitioning into the loving, understanding, and supportive wife Ron came to love as a young student at Bozeman Tech 20 years ago. Yes, she was worried about their finances, but she knew Ron was a talented guy and had always been a wonderful provider for their family. She knew Ron hadn't been happy with his job so maybe this would help him re-tool his career, re-define his goals, and chart a new and exciting path forward for himself and his family. Or, maybe they would be living in a van down by the river!

Ron didn't know what was next, but he always wanted to go back to school and finish his master's degree. He had finished all his course work but never finished his master's project for his degree because he was offered a job and decided he would return later. Maybe now was the time to do just that. A Master's in Information Systems (MIS) with a focus on leadership might be his ticket to better marketability, a better job, and a better life for his family.

He was haunted even as he started thinking about what he might do next. He had so many questions and so much self-doubt. He had just been fired. He let his family down. He let himself down by falling into a dysfunctional culture trap. He wanted to come back professionally and personally from this overwhelming feeling of abject failure. While he could see a possible path forward, he was professionally and psychologically wounded.

That night, Ron shared his idea about finishing his master's degree and Ellen loved the idea especially after she understood his severance package. She saw her husband as deeply disappointed and conflicted, but she also saw a man having a hint of hope with the idea of finishing his degree.

Somehow, someway their family would make it all work!

As it turns out, it was only a hint of hope. Ron didn't sleep well that night. The next day, he woke up depressed and confused. He beat himself up for letting down his family and embarrassing himself. He should have done something differently. He should have known better. He should have had the guts to do the right thing. He knew he let his team down. He felt like a man who had let everyone down. Ron Marshall was struggling as he waffled between embarrassment, depression, and self-pity.

Over the next few weeks, Ron barely left the house. He slept in almost every day, and on some days, he just laid there. His life lacked purpose. Sure, he was a dad and a husband, but he came to believe over time that his career was who he was. Ron Marshall was a talented, bright, innovative and creative technologist. He was a leader of teams: he was a visionary strategist, and respected colleague…until he wasn't any of those things anymore. All he was now was a stay-at-home bum with no job, little self-respect, and a roadmap straight to depression.

On Tuesday afternoon, Ellen came home early from work. No one seemed to be home. She climbed the stairs and walked into the bedroom to see her husband asleep, unshaven and wreaking of beer.

"GET YOUR BUTT OUT OF BED NOW!" she bellowed. "I love you, but self-pity is not becoming on you, Ron. Stop feeling sorry for yourself and start accepting reality. You are my husband and your son's father, and we need you to start acting like it!"

Ron wanted to reply in kind, but he held his tongue. He got out of bed, walked into the bathroom and saw himself in the mirror. Geesh!! Ellen was right, on all counts.

Lesson 9

 Everyone at one time in their lives needs a best friend who challenges them and gives them a dose of truth. This is the greatest form of love and support. When it happens to you, do not react, instead listen and learn and then thank that person who loves you enough to tell you the truth.

Chapter Ten: Shut up and listen

The next morning Ron woke up bright and early. Ellen noticed a look in his eyes she had not seen for quite a while. Ron showered and put on a coat and tie! Ellen was blown away. She was so used to the typical geek costume of khaki pants and a "schmedium" polo shirt with a stupid techy logo. She liked the new look. She loved her newfound husband! It seemed like years since she saw that glint in his eye. Before she knew it, she pulled him by his necktie back into their bedroom. Luckily, Freddy wasn't up yet.

Ron left with a hop in his step and drove to the Bozeman Tech campus to see Dr. Jack Rye, his former graduate advisor. Dr. Rye was an academic cowboy. He taught class during the week and roped steers over the weekend. He could lecture on Agile versus Waterfall Software Development and then tell you how to wield a branding iron on the backside of a steer. In fact, he even saw similarities for all the above. He believed in process and predictability, and he also believed in being flexible and to expect the unexpected. All applied to software development and roping a snot-snorting steer.

When Dr. Rye saw Ron, he immediately expected the unexpected. Why would Ron Marshall be dropping by?

"Ron Marshall! I am thrilled to see you," Dr. Rye shouted as he saw Marshall walking down the hall.

"Dr. Rye, I really need to see you. Do you have time for me?" Ron asked.

"I always have time for a former student who still sends me a Christmas card and those dark chocolate Polywogs every year," Rye enthusiastically replied. "Come in, Ron."

Dr. Rye looked older, but Ron probably looked a lot older than the kid who graduated almost 20 years ago as well.

"Dr. Rye, I lost my job and I need your help," Ron explained, getting right to the point. "I want to come back to school and finish my master's thesis."

"That is great, Ron! I knew someday you would come back." Rye leaned forward and put his hand on Ron's folded hands with a pat of comfort. Rye understood the uneasiness and disappointment of losing a job and he saw that Ron was equal parts excited and scared out of his mind.

"Ron, you understand the thesis will be reviewed and judged based on originality, innovative thought, and quality of written expression and execution." Rye took his glasses off and looked into Ron's eyes, "Do you know what you might want to do for your thesis?"

Marshall knew what he did not want to do. "I know I do not want to develop a corporate type project. I want to step outside my comfort zone and do something more entrepreneurial, something different and fun."

Dr. Rye had class starting in five minutes. "Ron how about you join me in class today? It's a class for second year graduate students and by coincidence it is called 'Entrepreneurial Management.' You in?"

Ron couldn't say yes fast enough. He entered the class and sat right up front just like he used to when he was Dr. Rye's student.

There was only one other student who sat in the front row. He wore Bozeman Tech basketball gear. "I'm Jason White," the student said as he extended his hand to meet the new guy in class. "Jason, I'm Ron, Ron Marshall. Nice to meet you."

Dr. Rye looked over the class and then looked at Ron with a mentor's proud smile. "Today we have a special guest, Mr. Ron Marshall. Ron has been a star in the corporate world of IT and most recently at Leola Data Systems," he explained to the class. "So, let's have some fun at Ron's expense and let him be our guinea pig today.

"Ron is looking at returning to school to finish his master's thesis but he's unsure of what direction he wants to go with this project. Ideas?"

Several students asked questions about Ron's background and if he had any experiences in the corporate world worth revisiting and possibly solving. Ron was polite and answered every question. Ron shared his background in managing projects around developing software and the challenges within a corporate environment.

Time was now running short in class. As Jason listened, he sensed Ron's willingness to continue answering questions, but most of the questions were really focused on what he could share to enhance the students experience, not help Ron. It was more about them than Ron.

As a young coach, Jason learned from Coach Woodward it was never about the coach unless you lost, then take the blame. Players should be given all the credit for the wins and the coach takes the bows and arrows for the losses. From those early coaching lessons, Jason learned how to connect with others by tuning into what THEY wanted, not what HE wanted.

Since Jason just left a meeting where he impressed Coach Woodward with a simple question, why not try a simple open-ended question again but this time with Ron Marshall. "Ron, what do you really want?"

Ron sat in stunned silence for 10 seconds, but it seemed longer, much longer. Jason had also learned to ask a question and be quiet. Silence meant thoughtful reflection and the possibility of truly connecting. It also created some awkwardness but allowed for the space of a well-thought out answer. He used this tactic in recruiting. *Be aware of what they want, not what you want. Ask a question then shut up and listen,* he heard in his head from Coach Woodward.

Ron Marshall then broke his silence after he looked into the distance and smiled, "I want to make a difference. I want to work with a team, not with siloed, selfish corporate types. I want to use my expertise to introduce quality throughout an organization. I want to help a team that wants to improve, that has the courage to look at what isn't working, and that is willing to change to get better. I've been in the tech world quite some time now, and frankly, I'd like to work with a team that is not full of geeks but maybe need a geek like me."

Dr. Rye smiled. Jason looked at Ron with the knowing grin of a little kid who had a secret and wanted to share it right now. Jason leaned toward Ron and whispered, "Let's talk after class."

Lesson 10

 LISTEN! Leaders are best defined by their ability to engage others and truly listen. Ask thought provoking questions.

Chapter Eleven: Recruiting diverse talent

After class, Jason pulled Ron aside and asked him if he knew anything about basketball. Ron loved basketball as a varsity high school player, and he wondered what the young coach might have in mind. Jason explained how Coach Woodward was looking for answers. Jason was fascinated by Ron's background as a corporate tech professional who knew how to build software, manage development teams and lead projects. Maybe, just maybe, Ron was the geek who could work with Coach Woodward and the team in an innovative and unique way.

It was certainly outside the box but maybe Ron could help them think differently and develop a different way to evaluate the team other than wins and losses. Jason wondered, *were there lessons he learned in the tech world that could apply to basketball? Maybe there was a combination of coaching expertise, innovative technology, and player buy-in that would change the way they went about preparing for opponents, evaluating on-floor execution, and measuring their own team's productivity.*

As Jason shared his notion, Ron wondered if he could provide an entirely new way to look at this losing team. He thought about how a quality assurance program might change the team's entire culture in a positive way. He certainly knew the pitfalls from a career full of learning from mistakes. Marshall knew what worked and what didn't work based on his corporate experiences and maybe this was the perfect place to apply all those lessons learned.

The bottom line was Ron Marshall needed to create a thesis and find a niche for an outside-the-box project to finish the final steps as he earned his master's degree. Jason needed to present a new way forward to Coach Woodward that would help this failing basketball program. Both were looking for answers and both needed each other.

This young coach was all in! This geek was all in!

Time to get started.

Lesson 11

 Watch carefully! Leaders are constantly looking for talent and recruiting talent, even in unexpected places. Jason realizes he has potentially found a talented team member. He immediately connects with Ron Marshall and recruits him to join his cause. Don't wait to start recruiting great talent. Even if your need is in the future, never stop identifying and recruiting great talent!

Chapter Twelve: Winning versus Success

Jason asked Ron to meet him that evening in the athletics conference room at 7PM. Ron arrived fifteen minutes early so he could figure out where he was going. As he walked down the long hallway, the building was full of energy because coaches from the different sports were in their offices and all seemed to be having boisterous conversations. It was loud!

All coaches are loud he thought to himself with a smile. Some coaches were calling recruits, others were plotting game strategies in staff meetings. It reminded Marshall of some of the Agile software meetings he ran that seemed free flowing but also energized and focused. He loved the frenetic pace he witnessed and the feeling of urgency and enthusiasm among the coaches.

In a strange way he felt more at home here than he felt in his last days, and even years, at Leola Data Systems. Maybe it was his excitement about doing something different, he thought to himself.

Marshall found the conference room and walked in with a big smile as Jason greeted him with an enthusiastic handshake. He felt like a geek, but heck he was a geek!

Jason had a Mountain Dew in front of him and offered Ron one from the fridge. Ron said, "Thanks, but not quite yet."

Jason was prepared. He shared with Ron the team's goal of getting focused on becoming a great defensive team.

He then went into an overview of the challenges the program faced and listed four key bullet points:

- Bozeman Tech had 17 straight losing seasons which was probably affecting the team's culture.
- The coaching staff had elevated the talent level of the team through recruiting at a higher level, but the current performance of the team did not match the level of talent on the team.
- Coaches are frustrated with the players and the players are frustrated with the coaches.
- Everyone is frustrated about losing.

"Jason, thank you," Ron interrupted. "I appreciate you sharing the challenges, but what do you and the coaching staff see as the opportunities?"

Jason thought for a moment, then went back to the whiteboard and listed what he believed to be their opportunities:

- Create a different and better winning culture
- Teach and coach better to elevate the talent
- Create greater individual and collective productivity

Ron challenged the young coach immediately, "Coach Jason, your first opportunity of creating a winning culture seems shallow to me." He stopped as he realized maybe his words were too harsh for such a young coach and such an immature relationship. "I'm sorry, Coach," he said.

Jason jumped in, "Sorry for what? I'm a freaking COACH Ron! We don't mix words here. I want your brutal honesty. Now, go on."

Ron laughed nervously but he got the message.

"To give you greater context, I just left a company that was focused only on the almighty dollar and that focus drove selfishness, greed, and a cover-your-ass mentality. 'Winning' (in air quotes) sounds more like my old company than a real 'Team' (in air quotes)," Marshall concluded.

Jason nodded and said, "Go on."

"Do you want to just win or is there something else that is more important?" Marshall asked.

The young coach pondered the question and he knew immediately this was the type of question the program needed to answer. He pondered for a moment longer. Maybe their focus on winning was self-centered because the coaches all knew that if they didn't win, they'd be fired. And, honestly, they all loved winning. They were all competitive.

Marshall interrupted his thinking, "Jason, why did you choose to become a coach?"

"I became a coach to help players in the same way my coaches helped me," Jason responded and then gulped his Mountain Dew.

"So, are you saying that it's more than winning for you? It's about helping your players be successful?" Marshall knew he was connecting with the young coach.

"Yea. Success both on and off the court and feeling like we are part of something bigger than ourselves," Jason expounded.

Ron and Jason drank an abundance of Mountain Dew and worked for several hours until suddenly they realized they had lost all track of time. It was 5:45 AM but it seemed like their meeting lasted maybe an hour. They had developed the beginnings of a plan and now they needed to share their ideas with Coach Woodward later that same morning.

Jason left and went to the coach's locker room to shower. *Youth has no alarm clock*, Ron Marshall thought as he left the building and headed home to get ready for his meeting with Coach Woodward.

Maybe it was the plan or maybe it was that fourth Mountain Dew, but Ron's energy was through the roof!

Lesson 12

 There is a big difference between being focused on winning versus being focused on success. What does success mean for you? Where are you focused?

Chapter Thirteen: Be memorable - the puker's Dad is exposed

Coach Jason had asked Ron Marshall to be at the Bozeman Tech basketball office by 10AM, but Marshall was ten minutes early and sat in the outer office shifting back and forth. He looked around at the player pictures on the office walls, and behind the reception desk there was a bigger-than-life mural of Coach Scott Woodward dominating the room. Ron felt out of place and a little intimidated. His last meeting in the corporate world ended in the loss of his job. He was about to face a new leadership team of college basketball coaches. He hoped this meeting would be different, but he had his doubts.

Marshall was a product of a corporate environment where sometimes honesty was not the best policy. In fact, sometimes it was better to shut up and hold your tongue, cover your ass, and play the game. Ron Marshall was about to enter an entirely new world, as he began learning last night with Jason.

Coach Woodward and Jason came around the corner. "Scott Woodward," as he extended his hand to greet Ron. "Coach Woodward, great to meet you. I am a fan!" Ron stood and immediately felt welcome.

"So, you are the one Jason was just telling me about!" Coach Woodward said with a laugh. Ron smiled and appreciated the joke to break the tension. Woodward then looked at Ron as they walked into the coach's conference room, "You look familiar."

"I go to a lot of your home games. In fact, I was there a few weeks ago for your home opener," Ron explained.

"Oh god. I'm sorry you had to suffer through that," Woodward sighed. "It was so bad some kid puked on the floor near the end of the game! Heck, I puked after the game!" Woodward said with a laugh.

"Ron, you have a family?" Woodward asked.

Ron was still laughing an uncomfortable chuckle, and then admitted sheepishly, "I am the puker's Dad."

Coach Woodward laughed until he cried. "What are the odds of that!?! Jason, you really know how to pick a consultant to help our program. At least we know he understands full-well how our team can make us all sick!" Now Ron laughed as the ice was broken, and he sensed an honesty and genuine connection with this coach. Hopefully, he was making the same positive first impression on Coach Woodward. He was.

"Ron, thank you for being honest and I hope the next time your son will not get sick from our lack of execution," Woodward stated matter of factly. Ron sensed the coach was switching gears. Now was the time to go to work.

Lesson 13

 Ron had the guts to be truthful in a very awkward situation, and Coach Woodward helped him feel comfortable. When you meet someone new, look them in the eye, shake their hand, and take a few moments to genuinely connect. That initial connection shows that you care about them as a person.

Chapter Fourteen: WHAT versus WHY

"Ron," Coach Woodward said, "as you know, we have a problem and Jason tells me that you have some ideas from your tech experience that might be able to help us."

"Coach, as a technology leader, we have had numerous large challenges through the years. I've used an assessment technique where we start with the problem or goal, then peel back the layers one by one to uncover the root causes. I think this same approach might be valuable here, but to do it right, it will take some time – probably several hours. Do you have the time?" Ron Marshall was all business as he looked Woodward right in the eye.

Woodward nodded approval, "I'm open all day, as this is an off day for us so no practice today. Ron, let's go."

"Let's start with some big picture discussion. Jason tells me you want to transform your team to become a great defensive team, and if everyone is focused, we can be successful," Ron Marshall stated in a steady, professional tone.

Coach Woodward heard the key word, "WE." He was immediately impressed with this geek!

Before Coach Woodward could respond, Marshall said, "Now that you have identified the what you want, we need to understand, why you want to be a great defensive team."

Coach Woodward leaned back in his chair looked up to the ceiling and muttered, "What versus Why. I get it."

Woodward understood the question better than most as he knew that average coaches can quickly identify what just happened and what went wrong, but great coaches look for the why. They want to understand why something happened and then diagnose the problem to fix it, so it doesn't happen the next time. *That is real coaching and I think Ron Marshall gets it*, he thought to himself.

"We need to be a great defensive team because we lack overall offensive skill sets. We are not going to outscore most teams," Woodward explained. "We need to be great at something and it is my belief we have exceptional lateral foot speed as a team. That means we can guard the man with the ball and defend the dribble drive."

"Let's brainstorm, Coach," Marshall responded. "How do we know if we are doing well defensively? Can we measure a great defender? Are there certain defined activities a great defender does within your system? Have you ever measured those specific activities?"

Coach Woodward liked the trajectory of this conversation. He stood up and yelled, "Jake, Jason, Donnie, Kevin get in here now!"

All the coaches rushed into the office and were told to sit down.

"Coach Marshall, ask them the same questions you just asked me," Woodward instructed excitedly and forcefully.

Ron was just called, 'Coach Marshall' by the head coach of his alma mater! *How cool is that?* he thought to himself.

Ron Marshall felt an excitement he had not felt in years. It was a moment in time he would never forget. It was that moment when circumstance and opportunity became one. It is that moment when his passion is aligned with his expertise and, he realized, he could make a difference.

"Coach Marshall", Ron liked that a lot!

Ron daydreamed for several seconds and now every coach was staring at him. Ron snapped back to reality and started the round of questions. The coaching staff was engaged, animated, excited. The brainstorming session went on for hours, but it seemed like 20 minutes. They ordered pizza and stayed on task until late into the night.

Just before midnight, Ron Marshall left the office tired but excited about the possibilities. Tomorrow morning, he would rise bright and early and meet with Coach Woodward one-on-one as the heavy lifting was about to begin.

Lesson 14

 So many people in business seem programmed to talk first and ask questions later. The more well-prepared questions are asked, the more it can lead to a better understanding of the needs and why those needs are so important to the success of the organization. Don't underestimate asking "Why?" It's a very powerful question that can help everyone gain clarity.

Chapter Fifteen: Introduction of People, Processes and Tools

At 7:30 AM sharp, Ron pulled out his notebook. "First, Coach, let's talk. I want to better understand your goals and what you perceive to be your weaknesses and strengths. I also want to provide more context around my experiences and how they might fit your team's needs.

"In the software business, we almost always start with an assessment because we learned that it's easy to make bad assumptions if you don't ask the right questions up front. Last night was most productive, but I want to drive last night's results into a more defined plan," Marshall set the tone early.

"With your permission I'd like to start with you, and in the next 24 hours, Jason and I have committed to interview every assistant coach individually and all of your players as well," Marshall stated with business-like authority.

"I believe we can draw some parallels to how we build high-quality software and successful business teams. I have always believed we could adapt to the ever-changing tech landscape to keep our teams competitive. I think it's just like you do every day as a head coach working hard to build your team and beat your competition," Marshall paused.

"Time-out," Woodward motioned with the 'T' of a coach wanting to get control of the game. "I asked for solutions, not questions."

"Jason informed me you wanted a plan and you are willing to try something different. I saw that in you and your staff last night. Look Coach Woodward, I am a fan and I believe in you personally. But the results from the last two seasons indicate your program might be ripe for accepting change. If you want READY, FIRE, AIM, I am not your guy," Marshall paused strategically to measure the man in front of him.

Coach Woodward was impressed with this businessman who was direct and seemed to have a path forward in mind. *What do I have to lose?* he thought to himself.

"OK, I'm all ears," Woodward replied, and now it was time for Ron to go to work.

Ron Marshall stood up and approached a whiteboard with diagrams all over it. "Can I erase some of these?"

"Jason, you captured these yesterday, right?" Woodward asked his young assistant coach. Jason nodded yes. Ron erased the plays on the board.

"The approach we use in the software industry starts with people, then looks at the process, and finally at the tools/technology." Ron drew a triangle with PEOPLE on top and PROCESS and TOOLS at the bottom corners of the figure, then continued.

"PEOPLE - One of the primary causes of poor performing teams is the people. Highly self-motivated people with the right aptitude and attitude combined with strong skills kick butt," Ron stated with the conviction of a coach. "In fact, in the tech world, 65-70% of the team's productivity is all about the people, 20-25% is from good consistent processes, and 10% or so is the tools. Losing teams exhibit poor communication, they lack trust in one another and their leaders, and they don't believe success is possible," Ron concluded with a deep breath and dramatic pause.

"These poorly run teams tend to depend on heroes for success, not teamwork. In fact, they build their culture around rewarding the heroes, which exacerbates the problem," Ron stated in a strong and measured tone.

"We need to explore your team of players and coaches and evaluate how well your team communicates. Are you building trust? Clearly, they want to win, but do they believe winning is possible? Do they trust each other, or do they only trust themselves?" Ron felt he was connecting with Coach Woodward.

"Jason shared with me your vision of building a culture of WE. He also shared with me your concern of the team being infected with the disease of ME." Ron Marshall could tell Coach Woodward was engaged as he sat up in his seat and smiled.

"Go on Ron. You've got my attention," Woodward confirmed he was indeed interested in what this geek had to say.

"Coach let's discuss the second corner of the triangle, Process," Ron Marshall continued. "Do we have a defined, consistent process for practicing and executing during a game? We want to ensure everyone understands the process and their specific role. That is key! In my business life both as a software developer and a leader, we want people cross-trained to handle different situations. This is also important with your team as you face injuries, disciplinary issues, etc.

"Also, how do we know if we are being consistent? Do we have any metrics, other than wins and losses to know if we are improving individually and collectively? In my business experience, these metrics tell us if what we are doing is working – or not. Plus, they provide unbiased feedback for everyone. Are we applying lessons learned from our key activities? Are we learning what's working and what's not, and are we adapting based on those lessons?" Ron was now energized as he pointed to the third corner. "TOOLS!" he yelled with a smile and a clap of his hands.

"Tools and Technology – Do we have the facilities and equipment needed to be most efficient during our practices? If not, what else could we use and what will it bring to us? Are we utilizing video to assess what went right and wrong in practices and games in real time? Are we using technology to our advantage when recruiting new talent? Are we using technology to better communicate across the organization?" Marshall was now on a roll and in his element. What he might not know or understand about being a college basketball coach or player he made up for in understanding the value of people, processes and tools.

"In my career, I've been brought into teams that needed help – you might say they needed a turn-around. Frankly, I lost my way with my last project, but I have learned from my mistakes. And maybe my experiences, both good and bad, can be valuable to you and your team," Marshall shared. "I've always started with an assessment to figure out where we are. After we know where we are and then determine where we want to go, we can finally build a roadmap to get there."

Coach Woodward stood up looked at the triangle on the board and said, "Ron and Jason, I like where this is going because I think similarly. I know that talent is the foundational key to success. How do we get started?"

Lesson 15

 Ron provided a vision for Coach Woodward with the three parts of his assessment triangle. It all starts with people regardless if it is basketball teams or business teams. Talent rules but the true role of a coach is putting the right people in the right place at the right time. The other two parts of the triangle do not matter if you can't get the people part right!

Chapter Sixteen: Be agile

Ron jumped in, "Coach, if I could, let me explain a couple of other things that I believe are critical to our success. When we build this roadmap to go from where we are to where we want to be, it needs to be executable, not some 50,000 ft. concept. We need to build pragmatic actions that we can start with right away.

"We will assess the team but understand we are building something new, and whether it be a software development team or a basketball team, we all need to learn new things. We need to change the way we've been doing things because, frankly, Bozeman basketball is not getting the results you want, or you wouldn't have me here today. So, we need to change, or we can expect more of the same," Ron said. "I love the Einstein quote, 'Insanity is doing the same thing over and over again and expecting different results.'

"Our initial work will be around setting and revising goals, establishing a plan, and then breaking it down into bite-size chunks. We will prioritize the chunks to find low-hanging fruit (aka, easy wins) that, in turn, should build confidence, motivate the team, and drive positive change. We need to raise the possibility of a different future, one step at a time," Ron Marshall was on a roll, but finally took a breath.

"How do we do that in a timely manner?" Coach Woodward asked. He was getting a bit nervous because this felt slow and heavy and he wanted results now. After all, he was a Ready, Fire, Aim guy.

"I thought about your team last night, Coach," Marshall continued. "My suggestion is we keep things 'agile' as we would say in the software development world. In other words, we start with small chunks and we build on those chunks and learn from our experiences, both positive and negative. Then we simply repeat the same processes that work. For the next set of small chunks, we identify new executable fundamentals if our team is ready for them. We build, we execute, we learn, and then we build more layers as we go."

Coach Woodward then interrupted, "So this is a continuous process where we teach and build on a foundation of small fundamental tasks or activities. We evaluate everything as we go. We share lessons learned from our failures and successes. We challenge ourselves individually and our team collectively to constantly find ways to improve. Is that it?" Woodward concluded.

"That's it, Coach Woodward!" Marshall responded, high fiving the head coach and Jason.

"My high school coach used to say, 'Every day in every way we get a little better.' So, we focus on the people first along with the fundamental processes. We look for the bite-sized chunks we can handle initially. Then we build on both to develop continuous improvement in practices and games," Ron Marshall concluded. Coach Woodward smiled and clapped his hands. Jason smiled as he watched his boss beam positive enthusiasm for the go-forward plan.

"Change is hard but if we do this right, communicate well, and listen to everyone, then I believe we will get buy-in to this new way of thinking and new way of executing. We have great kids and coaches and I am excited to work with you, Ron." Coach Woodward shook Ron's hand and then pulled him into a man-hug.

Lesson 16

 Even though Coach Scott Woodward and Ron Marshall come from different professional planets, there is always something to learn. There are always professional parallels and lessons learned that can bring value to a relationship and to a team. This chapter begins to show how two people from radically different walks of life can bring value to each other.

Chapter Seventeen: The process

Ron, Jason and Coach Woodward were now aligned. They decided both Ron and Jason would do all of the interviews in the next 24-48 hours and they settled on their basic list of questions:

Bozeman Tech Assessment Questions:

1. Why did you come here to coach/play?
2. What were you hoping to accomplish this season?
3. What are your goals for the team?
4. Where are we in achieving those goals?
5. What are your personal goals?
6. What's working well?
7. What's not working well?
8. What would feel like success over the rest of the season?
9. Do you think ALL coaches and players understand and are bought into the program's vision and plan?
10. Do you understand your role?
11. Do you have everything you need to execute your role?

Jason and Ron both would be looking for common themes to these questions, and they would document every response. Coach Woodward suspected there were some fundamental root causes that he hoped they could identify.

After their day off from practice, Coach Woodward called an all-players, all-coaches meeting prior to practice to explain what they were about to do and why they were doing it. The coaches and players seemed interested, engaged, and glad that they were trying something new. Ron was introduced as a consultant and was on point to do a team assessment with Coach Jason. The players were told to give them their time and undivided attention during the interviews. They expected complete honesty from every player and coach.

After practice, Jason and Ron worked around the clock. Jason interviewed most of the players as he had a trusting relationship as the youngest staff member. Coach Woodward felt the players would be more open with Jason. Ron interviewed all the coaches.

Both men understood the importance of this exercise as Christmas break was approaching and the immediate goal was to capture all the findings, develop their initial agile plan, and begin implementing that plan right after the players returned on December 26.

After doing the interviews and gathering the information, they first met as a two-man team to combine their results and identify common threads of positives and negatives.

While there were many diverse answers, Jason and Ron compiled the most common responses given as follows (13 players, 5 coaches):

1. Why did you come here to coach/play?

    o Of the 18 responses: (12) mentioned winning championships, every player (13) mentioned getting their degree, the next most common response, it was close to home (5). (Coach Woodward had a good reputation in the state and attracted good local talent)

2. What were you hoping to accomplish this season?

    o Everyone stated they had hoped to go to the NCAA tournament.

3. What are your goals for the team?
   o The majority re-stated the same as listed above.
4. Where are we in achieving those goals?
   o These responses were varied:
     ▪ (5) responded, "we are closer than some might think" and 4 of those responses were from coaches.
     ▪ (10) indicated the team was not close to becoming a championship level team and many of those responses included an opinion which did not believe that goal was 'realistic' as of today.
5. What are your personal goals?
   o All coaches, in some way, shared their need to grow professionally, make an impact on the players' lives, and to win. Most were also hoping to learn so they could grow in responsibility and eventually earn a head coaching position.
   o Players were more focused on grade point averages unanimously and a large majority (8) mentioned a greater need for balance in their lives.
6. What's working well?
   o Both Ron and Jason reported mostly silence and difficulty in answering this question regarding what was working well on the floor. Some mentioned that they felt like they were working hard, but not every teammate was and

they were frustrated by that. Most said nothing was working well other than academic progress.

7. What's not working well?

- o All coaches were player-focused in answering this question. One coach defined the staff's overall belief stating, "The players were not as dedicated as they needed to be as a group. They are not putting in the extra time outside of regular practice. And, frankly, many of the practices were not going well either."
- o A few of the coaches questioned the other assistants' commitment and dedication. There seemed to be a fair amount of in-fighting.
- o Some of the assistants questioned Coach Woodward's ability, although they felt somewhat optimistic since they are now trying something new.
- o All players were coach-focused in answering this question while raising the issues of flawed game plans, predictable offense, poor communication, and too much of an emphasis on just winning. In fact, one player, was very forceful in his belief around this last issue stated.
- o Players also identified wasted practice time due to long-winded instructions.
- o Several players questioned the commitment from their teammates and illustrated examples from recent games and practices.

8. What would feel like success over the rest of the season?

   o A few still had some hope of winning a championship and going to the NCAA tournament, but there were many who gave sarcastic comments.
   o The unanimous success barometer mentioned was to finish over .500 and make the conference play-offs (top four teams).

9. Do you think ALL coaches and players understand and are bought into the program's vision and plan?

   o While every single coach and player said they were bought in, in the next breath they could not consistently articulate the vision or the plan. Not one player or coach believed everyone else understood, let alone was bought into the program's vision and plan.

10. Do you understand your role?

   o Coaches indicated they basically knew their roles, but they could use a little more direction on how they could be even more productive and useful to the players and to Coach Woodward.
   o Players were even less definitive about understanding their roles. They all could give a general overview of their role, but when pressed to be more specific, not one player could clearly define their role in detail.

11. Do you have everything you need to execute your role?

    ○ Players had a recurring theme around their request for more individual skill development time with a coach every day.

    ○ Coaches generally felt they had what they needed but the younger coaches felt the program was not leveraging technology to gain an advantage.

From this detailed information, Jason and Ron were ready to organize these findings and their recommendations into an Assessment report.

Lesson 17

 Any time you want to change the culture of an organization, you better have a clear understanding of where you are currently. If you ask the right questions and your team provides honest input, you can begin to identify areas for improvement while beginning the process of changing your culture. You must be very careful in asking the questions to ensure you are not unexpectedly leading them to your desired answer. Be sure to look for the truth and minimize your biases in your questions and when summarizing their answers.

Chapter Eighteen: Accepting the truth

Jason and Ron walked into Coach Woodward's office the afternoon of December 22. "Coach, before we share the full Assessment report, I want to share a sensitive point," Jason stated. "As you know, we interviewed all our coaches and players. We have captured every conversation, but there was one specific conversation I want you to focus on," Jason explained.

"One of our objectives was to keep the results anonymous so everyone felt safe to give their honest input. However, when you read the report, I think you'll be able to associate some of the comments to specific people. And, some of these findings aren't pretty," Jason shared, uncomfortably.

Finally, Coach Woodward interrupted, "Listen guys, I asked you to put together an honest report and I expect there is bad news. If there wasn't, we probably wouldn't need this assessment. So, just tell me what you need to tell me."

"Coach, we asked the players questions around how we could get better and while we've captured all of the player's comments, Brian Clark was able to provide what I believe to be a brutally honest and mature approach to what we really need in order to be successful both on and off the court," Jason continued.

Brian Clark was a starting forward for the team and his Dad had played for the Lakers. Brian had a lifelong history around the game at the highest levels. He was smart, thoughtful, and perceptive. Brian never mixed words and was seen as a team leader.

"I asked Brian, 'What do you think the team needs to do to be more productive and become more successful?'"

Recounting Brian's answer, Jason swallowed hard and paused for a second. Then he shared, "Coach is a fraud when it comes to what he says and how he acts sometimes. I love Coach but think about how he challenges us. Everyday Coach challenges us to concentrate on the little things. He talks about executing the little things versus winning and losing. He says winning takes care of itself when you prepare well and execute the little things. Don't worry about wins and losses, instead trust each other and trust the process. Yet, at the end of every timeout, we say '1-2-3 WIN!' That is an insult to me and every player. Doesn't he know we all want to win? He teaches us to trust each other and trust the process, yet all he is really focused on is winning."

Jason stopped reading as he watched his head coach drop his head into his hands and covered his eyes. There was still one last thing Brian had to share and so Jason read on, "If trusting the process is really where Coach Woodward is focused, then why can't we all focus on the same things, and then maybe winning will actually begin to take care of itself?"

Coach Woodward stood up and looked out his window that overlooked their practice facility. There was Brian Clark in the gym working on his game. Woodward knocked on the window and got Brian's attention. The head coach waved to Clark, smiled, and gave him a thumbs up!

Lesson 18

 Jason delivers a hard message to Coach Woodward. Notice Coach Woodward never challenged the perception of himself as a 'fraud'. As a leader, ask for the truth and be prepared to hear the truth.

Chapter Nineteen: The report

Coach Woodward then turned to Jason and Ron, who handed him the Assessment report. "Coach, we're excited about what we've been able to put together in such short order. It's not perfect, but it's a good start. With Ron's corporate background doing these types of assessments, I think we've also developed some good recommendations that can help us. We hope you think so, too."

"Thanks guys," Woodward said. "I like how this has gone so far and I look forward to reading it." Woodward took the document and, realizing it was several pages long, packed it into his laptop bag. His head was still spinning from what Brian Clark said, and he wanted some quiet time to read through and absorb the material. He knew that the pending Christmas break would afford him ample time. As Ron and Jason headed out for break, they all shook hands and gave each other a man-hug, then wished each other a Merry Christmas.

Assessment Report
Bozeman Tech Basketball

Compiled for: Coach Scott Woodward

Executed and Prepared By: Ron Marshall, Consultant/ Graduate Student and Jason White, Director of Basketball Operations

Summary: The Bozeman Tech basketball coaches and players were interviewed between December 19-20. The goal was to determine the honest views of the coaches and players regarding the direction of the program. Here are the overall trends:

1. The players and coaches identified the team goals as being:
   - .500+ team
   - Conference champions
   - NCAA Tournament participants

2. A majority of respondents acknowledged the team is not near to achieving any of those goals as it stands today.

3. In many cases, the players and coaches could not identify even one area that was 'working well'.

4. Players tended to blame coaches and coaches tended to blame players for their lack of success. Some blamed Coach Woodward.

5. There is confusion around the program's vision and plan at all levels of the organization.

6. While team roles as coaches and players can be generally defined, those roles seem to lack clarity and depth of understanding. Accountability for performing those roles is inconsistent.

7. Communication, or lack thereof, was a very common theme. Most indicated it was an area that needs immediate improvement, specifically with and from the head coach.

8. The team wants to improve their skill levels and wants time available to focus on improving individually with coach supervision.

9. Players also made multiple mentions of coaches talking too much in practice. They would like to see the practices with more productive time spent working on their game and the team's skill sets versus verbal instruction.

10. Both coaches and players feel the program could better leverage technology to improve communication and efficiency during practices, games, and in the team video sessions.

11. The players did identify their collective academic commitment as a great team achievement and recognized the coaches for their focus and support in this area. They also believed there was still room for improvement.

RECOMMENDATIONS:

1. **Terminology** - The terms vision, mission, goals, values and culture are confusing to the players and coaches, so let's start by better defining these terms. This will help tremendously with some of our team communication challenges while getting everyone on the same page. The following is based on the interviews and inputs with ALL coaches and players and direct input from Coach Woodward:

   o Vision – (the desired future state of the team) **Become the most selfless teammates and most positive and productive members of our college community.**

o Mission – (what the team does today to achieve success)

- On the floor, success is measured by our commitment to defend our opponents in one on one matchups and collectively as a team.
- We are selfless team members who focus on our defensive process and challenge each other as coaches and players to continuously improve.
- Off the floor we commit to being attentive and productive students and classmates.
- We are examples of leadership and accountability for our campus community.

o Goals – (as defined during the interviews)

- Achieve a team GPA over 3.2 for the semester
- Finish over .500 for the first time in 17 years
- Be the top defensive team in the conference based on defensive efficiency stats
- Earn a spot in the conference play-offs

o Values – (what we believe and how we act as an organization. Our values drive our culture.)

- ACCOUNTABILITY- everyone has the responsibility and authority to achieve their personal goals and frankly, to help

others achieve their goals. Everyone has the responsibility to respectfully challenge each other when anyone is not living up to their stated goals.
- HONESTY ALWAYS!
- CONTINUOUS IMPROVEMENT individually and as a team.
- POSITIVE SUPPORT of each other.
- DIVERSITY – We believe diversity makes us stronger, better teammates, and better citizens.

2. **Communication** - We recommend weekly individual player and coach meetings with Coach Woodward to better connect, communicate, and track progress individually and collectively around their specific role.

3. **Efficiency** – We recommend a more focused approach to improving communication with all players and coaches. Teach in shorter sound bites. Use 'economy of language' for easy to understand direction and 'to-the-point' communication techniques. We recommend less talk in practice which will drive higher productivity.

4. **Technology** – We recommend the use of technology to better teach in practice and games and to provide the team and individuals unbiased feedback. Also, leverage modern technology to improve team communication (Ex. group texts, etc.).

5. **Governance** - In business we use a term called 'Governance'. Governance ensures that everyone

understands their role and their ability to make decisions. Coach Woodward needs to be the Governance lead. We recommend he document (in writing) the specific role for each assistant coach so everyone clearly understands their authority to coach, assess, and adjust in practice and in games. This covers everything from recruiting, planning and executing practices, adjusting during the games, and analyzing performance data post game. The same applies for all players. We recommend Coach Woodward or key assistants clearly document every player's role (in writing), and that these roles be reinforced by the coaches and fellow teammates.

6. **Buy-In** is critical. This is a cultural statement. We see examples of players and coaches who act bought-in when the head coach is there but act differently when he's not. To be successful, everyone needs to be fully on board. We recognize there is work to be done here. To achieve buy-in, we recommend the following:

   o Publish, reinforce, and memorize (all coaches and players) the vision, mission, goals, and core values.
   o Display them prominently in the locker room.
   o At each team meeting, invite players/coaches to tell everyone what they have accomplished, where they are falling short, and how they can better hold themselves accountable. Buy-in takes place with personal accountability first.
   o To give the team some specific goals that they can achieve and celebrate, we recommend

utilizing a Career Best Effort (CBE) Strategy. CBEs are key behaviors that do not require special skill but do require concentration and effort. We suggest the coaches develop a short set of CBEs that are common across the entire team, primarily focused on building defensive success. In addition, we recommend that each player and coach review and create their own CBEs which holds them individually accountable for their behavior.

o We also recommend a better-defined plan to manage in-game situations. We believe halftimes need to be more inclusive, which allows the players to begin self-correcting. We recommend using innovative technology with the goal of more pro-active coaching.

7. **Simplicity** is a critical component of our plan. Some teams lose focus because there are too many initiatives, and therefore, none are performed in a quality manner. We often see this in business as these teams and companies get enamored with the latest buzz words and end up chasing their tails. The KISS ('Keep it simple stupid') principle really applies here. We recommend the team focus on being good to great at 2-3 things versus trying to be good at all things.

8. **Culture of Truth** - We need to be truthful with each other and be open and willing to hear bad news as well as good news. The coaches and players need to be open. This is not a democracy. The coaches are in charge, but to have great team culture and

buy-in, it's imperative that we allow everyone to voice their ideas and opinions. But, when the coach/player in charge has listened, and when a final decision is made, everyone needs to be on-board, whether they agree or not.

9. **Agile** - Lastly, we need to implement change smartly and quickly using agile principles. We are in the middle of a basketball season and cannot afford to try and eat the whole elephant at once. Even when drafting the Vision, Mission, Goals, and Values, we don't need a fully thought through approach. We need the foundational pieces on which we can build. For the initial plan, we need to quickly and thoughtfully select the low hanging fruit (easy to implement items that will provide good results) and prioritize these first.

"Whew!" Coach said out loud once he finally finished reading. This was a lot to absorb. As he read the report, he found himself having to stop several times to re-read sections. He wondered how his youngest assistant coach and a freakin' geek who barely ever played basketball could come up with these recommendations! He waffled between feeling overwhelmed, ashamed that he hadn't seen what was going on, and angry at himself because after all, he was the head coach who should know what he's doing.

He paused and took a few deep breaths to calm himself and clear his head. Then, he re-read it once again. This time, he began feeling a bit excited about the possibilities of building a better culture and team. It was a lot to absorb and process. It was hard to hear all of this and realize that he could have been doing a much better job all along. But at the same time, it was exciting that they had some fresh new ideas that might gel this team and help propel them forward.

Lesson 19

 Often our greatest lessons come after we lower our self-defense mechanism. When you are confronted with difficult news about your performance, take a few moments to breathe so you can open yourself to a better you.

Chapter Twenty: Building a team while creating a family

Christmas was almost here, and these assessment results were a lot to chew on. Coach Woodward was keen to take a few days off and think about things, but he also wanted to unwind and clear his head. There was one problem, he didn't really have anyone he could talk with about all of this.

Woodward, while outwardly social and well-liked by almost everyone (except his boss), really had no life outside of basketball. His team won their last game before the break and now stood 3-6 on the season. It was December 23rd as he sat in his two-bedroom ranch-style rental. It was spartan, nothing hanging on the walls, and hand-me-down furniture from the 80s. The only thing he had that was nice was his 60" LED TV.

He and his players would have off through December 26 to go home and be with their families. He, on the other hand, really did not have a family. His parents had divorced when he was eleven, and he rarely ever heard from his alcoholic father. His mother raised him alone, but sadly passed away from breast cancer when he was only twenty-two. He still missed her, especially during the holidays. He was an only child, and now was a lonely man without his assistants and team on campus.

Coach sat and watched the last game tape with a cold glass of Christmas cheer in the form of a Captain and Coke. While he watched, he thought back to the meeting with Jason and Ron. Their new plan would be hatched the evening of the 26th during their first practice back on campus after the break. Coach Geek, as he was now known, and Jason worked day and night over the last week to deliver their go-forward plan.

Woodward was getting over his shame and was quickly getting all-in on the new direction. He had always been a bit of a gunslinger and was not afraid to take chances. He thought Coach Geek was nerdy, quirky and detailed to a fault, but he was also brilliant.

His doorbell rang and Woodward looked out the window. A light blue Prius with a lady and kid in a car-seat was parked in his driveway. He opened the door and there stood Coach Geek, sporting khakis and a natty hoody that said, 'ORACLE' on it.

"Hi Coach, I wanted to drop by and give you some follow-up information on how we can hold each other accountable when the team returns on the 26th," Marshall said.

"Awesome!" Woodward exclaimed.

Coach Geek handed him a piece of paper with instructions on how to download a SharePoint app. Woodward stared at it and look at Marshall, "What the hell is this?"

"It's SharePoint, which is a cloud-based service that helps organizations share and manage content, knowledge, and applications. I used it in my last job. This tool will help us empower teamwork, quickly find information, and collaborate and communicate across the organization. It provides a tool for us to track the players from their baseline performance on the 26th to everyday improvement throughout the season. This will be a work in progress as we learn how to better communicate as an organization. It's not quite finished yet, so just play with it and tell me what you think," Coach Geek explained.

"Come in a minute, Ron. Oh, and ask your family to come in. I have something for you." Woodward looked out the window as Coach Geek waved to his wife to come in.

"Coach Scott Woodward, this is my wife Ellen and my son Freddy," Marshall said with pride.

Woodward gave Ellen a hug and welcomed her to the Bozeman Tech basketball family. Then he turned to little Freddy and said, "Hey! You're the PUKER!" They all laughed.

Coach Woodward asked them all to sit down, then excused himself and ran out of the room and into the garage.

The Marshall family sat in silence. Ellen looked around at a typical bachelor pad that felt a bit sad with limited furniture - no character, and a few dishes in the sink. The house was clean but devoid of any personality except for a Charlie Brown Christmas Tree that sat on an end table with three ornaments. It looked lonely.

Ellen looked at Ron and he nodded knowingly, "Yes, go ahead," he said.

Coach Marshall came back into the room with Bozeman Tech shirts, shorts, hoodies, sweatpants, and a green and gold basketball for Freddy.

"Oh, my goodness!" exclaimed Ellen. "Freddy, look at that ball!" Freddy jumped off the couch and grabbed the ball. He instantly dribbled across the living room and into the kitchen. The kid was STOKED!

"Scott, this is so awesome. Thank you!" Ron said.

"Coach Marshall, would you join us for Christmas Eve dinner and church service tomorrow night? We would love to have you join our family!" Ellen asked.

"Wow, really? You bet. What should I bring?" Scott asked.

"You just bring yourself," Ellen answered. "Tomorrow we look forward to seeing you around 5PM?"

"SOLD!" Scott replied in his enthusiastic coach's voice.

The Marshall family hugged Coach Woodward then headed out to their car. Woodward stood in the doorway and watched. He smiled the smile of a grateful man who really wanted a family. This was a man who could coach a team but didn't know how to really be part of a family.

The next night Woodward got a lesson on what it meant to be a loyal, and loving husband and father. He watched Ron and Ellen hold hands. Freddy was respectful of his parents and was outwardly affectionate toward both his mother and father. He saw and heard what a true family looked like and felt like.

Later that night at the church service as 'Oh Holy Night' echoed off the stained glass of the old Gothic style church, he prayed. Not the prayer of a coach looking for his next win or to save his job. Instead, he said a prayer of thanksgiving for Ron, Ellen, and Freddy. He thanked God for leading him to Ron and his family.

He ended his prayer with one last request on this Christmas Eve, "Please don't let Freddy puke at anymore of our games!" Coach Woodward sat down and smiled. "Merry Christmas," he whispered to himself.

Lesson 20

 There is a big difference between interacting with someone and connecting with someone. Coach Woodward tried to connect with the Marshall family with team gear, while Ellen made the decision to open the Marshall home to Coach Woodward even before the gifts were given to her family. Both made the effort to connect, not just interact. In your organization, are you connecting or just interacting?

Chapter Twenty-One: Build, break, battle, bond

Coach Woodward woke up early the next morning excited, as his players were returning to campus. He went to his office to prepare for the first practice back from Christmas break. First, he led a staff meeting with his coaches and he reviewed their plan. Everyone was excited to re-engage the team with their new focus and plan.

It was December 26th and every player reported to the gym, on time, shirts tucked in and ready for the new year. They all knew the next 10 days would be the most challenging practices of the season. This part of the season was a time to review the past and learn from their pre-conference games. It was critical now to improve today and every day if they were to contend for a conference championship. The new focus would be on continuous improvement both on and off the floor.

Bozeman Tech was 3-6 on the season and there was much work to be done. Coach Woodward sent them on Christmas break with a message, "Come back ready to work. Come back with an open mind. Come back ready to be coached like you've never been coached before."

The whistle blew and Woodward ran to center court. Everyone followed his lead including the newest member of the coaching staff, Ron Marshall. Marshall wanted to throw up. He was so nervous, but Freddy had already baptized the court for him just a few weeks ago.

Marshall could see Ron was pasty white. He remembered Freddy from the earlier game, and he hoped Ron wouldn't spew like his son.

"Welcome back guys! Tonight, we begin our season anew. Tonight, and every day from now until season's end we get better. Tonight, we make changes," Coach Woodward set the tone.

"CHANGES!" he said with force. "Here is our plan. First understand one thing, we are 3-6 and I believe we are better than that record." Then he challenged every player one by one, "Do you believe we are better than our record?" Every single player and coach responded with, "Yes, sir."

"Good." Woodward stopped and paused for what seemed like a minute looking at each young face as they all wanted to hear what was next. "How many of you played Fortnite over break?" Every player raised their hands. "How many of you won?" Danny Kellar sheepishly raised his hand.

"I played with my little brother and finished ahead of him," Kellar said, barely audible as his teammates laughed.

"Look, I am not going to pretend to be a Fortnite expert, but you have to BUILD to win, right? You sometimes need to BREAK things in your path, BATTLE to survive and hopefully, BOND with someone you trust." The players all nodded and were kind of impressed Coach Woodward knew anything about Fortnite.

"Today, we begin the process of building new successful habits and setting higher expectations while breaking old bad habits. Starting today, we are preparing for battle by creating a bond within our team in different ways." Woodward could see the excitement in the players' eyes.

"I have added a graduate assistant coach to our staff. You will call him 'Coach Marshall.' He is working on his master's degree and he will be around every day. His role is to evaluate everything you do in practice and everything we do as a team," Woodward explained. "Coach Marshall is the electronic eye of the program and our quality coach. His job is to assess us, test us, and monitor our improvement every single day. Our coaching staff will break our bad habits and help us build new ones. We will prepare for battle in a different way through the initiatives we are instituting starting tonight."

Coach Woodward continued, "Before I introduce the newest member of our staff, I want to establish our Vision, Mission, and Team goals."

"Our Vision – Become the most selfless teammates and most positive and productive members of our college community.

Our Mission – On the floor, success is measured by our commitment to defend our opponents in one-on-one match ups and collectively as a team. We are selfless team members who focus on our defensive process and challenge each other as coaches and players to continuously improve. Off the floor, we commit to be attentive and productive students and classmates. We are examples of leadership and accountability for our professors and campus community."

Woodward then stopped and asked if there were any questions. He continued, "Based on your input, we have clearly established four goals:

1. Achieve a team GPA over 3.2 for the coming semester

2. Finish over .500 for the first time in 17 years

3. Be the top defensive team in the conference based on defensive efficiency stats

4. Earn a spot in the conference play-offs

"Tonight, we begin the process of working toward those goals - which all of you defined - as we start BUILDING new habits! You in?" Everyone answered Woodward's question with a unified, "YES, SIR!"

"Coach Marshall, they are all yours," Woodward stated.

"Hi guys, I'm a geek." The players laughed as Marshall swayed nervously back and forth. "After practice tonight I will meet with you to explain how we will use our new SharePoint website to communicate better. You all shared during our assessment that you wanted the staff to improve communication with you. This is one way we will do exactly that," Ron stated.

"This is one part of our new strategy to apply technology to help us improve and be successful both on and off the court, but it's important that we are all on-board with this new program. As we develop new habits, I will be keeping an eye out for some of the old non-productive habits. When I see them, Coach Woodward asked me to point them out to you, both players and coaches. It's hard to break out of old bad habits and develop new ones, so I will also be working with the coaches to reinforce what's working well and where we can continue to improve," Coach Marshall explained. "Back to you, Coach Woodward."

"OK guys. Let's get to it! It's time to practice," Coach Woodward said, then he blew his whistle and sneakers squeaked across the court.

Lesson 21

 Connecting with your team can be a challenge. Coach Woodward stepped outside his comfort zone by referencing Fortnite as a bridge to get his team's attention. This allowed him to share the vision and mission directly with the team. In many organizations, the message gets lost as they try to communicate from the managers on top, down to the people who do the real work. Woodward connected the entire organization and shared the expectations in language that everyone could understand.

Chapter Twenty-Two: The technology arrives

Later that evening, several packages from Amazon arrived at Ron Marshall's house. Ron and Jason ordered new basketball technology 'toys' for Christmas to complement their strategy for better accountability, measurement, and communication.

The packages were waiting for Ron when he got home from practice and he opened the boxes like a kid at Christmas! This was fun!

Now he had to figure out how to get them working before tomorrow's practice. He spent the evening and late into the night connecting and setting up the devices. He was creating a set of tools tailored to each player. The players were going to love this. Heck, he loved it!!

At practice the next day, Coach Woodward gave Coach Marshall the floor. "Guys, a few super-cool belated Christmas presents have arrived for us! On the rack are special basketballs, each with your own name on them, that you will use for all your dribbling and shooting drills. These are your personal 'Connected' basketballs. Go find yours and come right back." Ron could see excitement in their eyes.

Every player sprinted over to the rack bumping into each other to get there first. They all picked up their own ball. One by one they came out bouncing the ball is if they just got a new toy. Marshall sensed their excitement but warned them, "This is not a toy. It is a tool and we will use this tool every day moving forward. For now, just know this ball will record every dribble you make, every pass you throw, and every shot you take. We will record everything you do. We will evaluate your performance with your ball, in real time."

Now the players were more retrospect. They suddenly realized this new tool could either lead to reward or failure and it was on them as individuals to accept responsibility for how they utilized their 'Connected' ball. Marshall also introduced an app called, The Player Tracker. It maps a basketball court in 3D. The app charts all player movement on the court in real time and provides historic data from previous workouts for comparison.

Coach Woodward then pulled out the team's new practice jerseys. Each player got a practice jersey with their number and name on it. The team put on the new jerseys immediately, as they loved new gear!

"Ok, now feel the small pocket in the jersey just above your heart. Feel that small sensor?" Marshall could see their excitement. "That sensor will measure your heart rate and will help us track not only your physiological reaction to stressors such as running, but also high-pressure game situations. It also has a special motion sensor built in, which allows us to analyze your shooting form and shot mechanics. It transmits shot metrics to our mobile phone or iPad. During your individual workouts we can analyze your jump height, rotation, hang-time, shooting form, and acceleration in real time."

"With this sensor and The Player Tracker app, we can also easily evaluate where you are on the floor in real time. It will measure your spacing from one player to the next on offense and defense. It will measure your effort as we sprint the floor on a fast break or run back to stop our opponents," Marshall paused for effect. "Every effort you make will now be measured and graded for quality. That is my job, to measure and report this data so the other coaches can evaluate our individual and team quality and productivity."

"Holy crap," said Danny Kellar. "We are living in a different basketball world."

"This is our own little metrics-driven basketball world. WE will build it and own it. WE will measure our own productivity. WE will break old habits. WE will battle for what WE want TOGETHER AS A TEAM!" Coach Woodward summarized it all up as he saw buy-in from his players.

Kellar exclaimed, "We have a Coach Geek!" Ron Marshall loved it and nodded approval as the players laughed and high fived their new quality coach.

The coaches started the drills and Coach Geek watched the data upload in real-time to his SharePoint server. There was a lot of data rolling in fast. Coach Geek was like the Wizard of Oz but what would be hiding behind the curtain?

Lesson 22

 One way to show your team that you are investing in them is to leverage new tools and technology to help them succeed. These tools can measure their individual and collective improvement over time. Consistent practice of the right habits results in consistent execution. Technology can measure your productivity, identify areas for improvement, and show the team how they are improving. It's objective and unbiased and gives them all an opportunity to celebrate their successes. Are you investing in your team, or is everyone stuck doing things the same old way on archaic systems?

Chapter Twenty-Three: The balancing act

Coach Woodward knew he was heading down a road with many forks. His challenge was balancing the data while avoiding paralysis by analysis. He knew he could better hold his players accountable with all the data Coach Geek compiles, but how could he also give them freedom to play?

Woodward knew there had to be a balance. Some data would need to be shared with the players while other data was strictly for the coaches.

Woodward and his staff held many meetings as they were adjusting to their new reality of data-driven evaluation and decision-making. Coach Woodward insisted that the players well-being both mentally and physically came first. Then, their performance or, even better, their improved performance needed to be effectively communicated regularly, clearly, and concisely.

Each player met with the head coach during the first few days back from Christmas break. As part of their new culture to be more inclusive and ensure they were all moving forward together, he and Coach Geek agreed on three questions as part of their assessment phase for both offense and defense:

1. How do you want to be evaluated defensively/offensively?

2. What do you see as our three most important defensive/offensive principles that drive team success?

3. How would you hold yourself and your teammates accountable for these specific principles?

The answers ranged from the typical coach speak to innovative outside-the-box ideas. One player suggested video game-like feedback that was immediate and had consequences on the spot. He suggested practices include immediate rewards when success was achieved individually and/or collectively, depending on the drill. On the flipside, if someone or a group failed, they would be eliminated on the spot until given a new chance to re-enter the drill/scrimmage/game, much like a video game.

Woodward loved that concept. It ensured a high level of competition and accountability. With this approach, players would take more ownership in their own performance and their teammate's performance as he envisioned an inter-connected team of individuals all held to the same expectations.

This concept of tracking all competition could drive success data for each player based on their practice performance. In other words, if you won a drill or even an individual match up, the staff could keep track of which players consistently found ways to win a drill or beat an opponent.

Another player suggested more immediate video feedback both during and after practice. He wanted video clips to be shown immediately in practice along with the coach's verbal reminders. He wanted video clips sent to him so he could review them after practice to better understand where he was making mistakes and where his teammates were making mistakes. He wanted to learn both in real-time and to review after practices and games.

Jason would be on point as he was a video software wiz. The goal was to send each player 3-5 short video clips to reinforce behaviors the coaches were looking for. He could mark specific clips in practice and upload them to SharePoint immediately after practice.

Another player had shared that halftime was only half productive. He raised the issue that players sit for 5-10 minutes waiting for the coaches to come into the locker room. Why couldn't Jason send video clips at halftime for team review prior to the coaches coming in? They could easily do it at home with their locker room monitors, and at away games, they could send the video clips to their phones.

If Jason could figure it out quickly, they would implement this video strategy in practice as a proof of concept. If successful, this strategy could prove to be a game changer. The coaching staff knew the challenge was to manage the balance between hands-on activities and the need to stop and learn.

From the assessment interviews and follow-up meetings, the coaching staff captured some key activities they wanted to implement, but they prioritized the most important and low-hanging fruit around personal accountability. They decided to start with what they called a Career Best Effort (CBE) Strategy. Coach Geek explained this new CBE process as a technique to develop specific measurable activities that would only take concentration and effort but no special talent. It was an approach that he used in the software world that allowed the team to see themselves improve every week. Where basketball was generally only measured in wins and losses, they envisioned a future where they could measure and actually feel success even if they lost, but as long as they improved their CBEs. They knew this might be a stretch, but they needed a way to celebrate some successes even in team defeat.

Coach Geek challenged the coaches and players to begin to think in terms of simple actions that lead to success both on and off the floor. As they developed specific roles for each player, Coach Woodward and his assistants met with each of them to define a set of CBEs that were tailored to that role. For their big guys, they developed defensive positioning CBEs and rebounding/block off CBEs. For their guards, they had a pressuring the ball CBE and off-ball defensive positioning CBEs.

They also asked each player to develop CBEs to improve their personal lives. This was about growing personal accountability while building successful habits on and off the court.

Each of the assistants and Coach Woodward also developed CBEs. If they were going to ask their players to do something, they better step up themselves.

Woodward could see the culture was beginning to change. It was more inclusive, less top-down driven, and more focused on individual growth. The players seemed energized and so was their head coach.

Lesson 23

 The people who do the job often have the best ideas to improve the team and organization, but they are rarely asked. Leaders of organizations who truly want change are willing to listen to those who perform the jobs.

Chapter Twenty-Four: Danny Kellar's Career Best Effort plan

Danny Kellar was a senior leader on the team. He was a small-town kid from Pocatello, Idaho. He knew the meaning of hard work and was excited about this new path forward. Kellar had never been part of a winning team at Bozeman Tech. He liked Coach Woodward and respected the coaches and he believed this team would now break their history of failure. Seventeen straight losing seasons were in his rear-view mirror. Kellar was determined to make history. This was his last shot.

Every player was challenged to come back the next day with a plan for personal success. They were to make 4-5 statements in present tense with actions for success that were easily quantified. Danny took this homework seriously. He thought about his personal and academic goals. He thought through exactly what he needed to do to be a better student, friend, teammate, and son. He decided on four statements and a simple way to measure them and hold himself accountable:

I attend class every day (Danny had 15 credit hours that required 17 hours of class time/week including a lab. He listed a spot for every hour of class time, and would mark them off one at a time, every day.)	(1) (2) (3) (4) (5) (6) (7) (8) (9) (10) (11) (12) (13) (14) (15) (16) (17)

I ask or answer at least two questions in each of my classes to stay engaged. (Danny wanted to be more engaged in his classes, and would mark off each hour of class time when he successfully reached his goal)	(1) (2) (3) (4) (5) (6) (7) (8) (9) (10) (11) (12) (13) (14) (15) (16) (17)
I connect with and recognize ten classmates each week (not team members) for their extra effort in class. (Danny wanted to better connect with people not in his athletics focused world.)	(1) (2) (3) (4) (5) (6) (7) (8) (9) (10)
I call home 3x/week to connect with Mom, Dad or my little brother. (Danny came from a broken home and still had a little brother in high school. He wanted to be a better son and brother.)	(1) (2) (3)

Danny had a plan and he was excited to share it with his coaches and teammates. It was simple but he knew if he held himself accountable, it would lead to greater success in class, better relationships with his family, and expand his sphere of friends.

Lesson 24

 Danny shows the willingness to embrace change and give it a try. As you drive change in your organization, who are the internal leaders who will not only be an advocate but also a member of the change club?

Chapter Twenty-Five: Activities, activities, activities

After several days of practices with the new equipment and strategies, players seemed more engaged and self-aware. The coaching staff was focused on specific fundamental behaviors. As they focused on fewer things, it gave them deeper clarity and allowed them to be more consistent in holding their players accountable. Because of this focused attention, the players were adjusting and beginning to look at these same behaviors and were starting to self-correct. The coaches and team were working night and day as there were no academic classes during this time of Christmas break. The rest of the student population would not return to campus until mid-January. Since there were no outside distractions, it allowed them to focus on their new approach to basketball.

Each day consisted of a 7AM coaches 'Stand-Up' meeting where they each shared what they accomplished the day before, what they intended to accomplish today, and any roadblocks in their way. In addition, the coaches shared any relevant experiences and lessons learned from practice. This was a practice they learned from Coach Geek and his experience leading Agile software teams. The coaches also planned their morning one-hour class with the players, which was required in the team room. In those meetings, Coach Geek opened each morning meeting with a review of the previous day's productivity stats in practice. The players and coaches reviewed their CBEs, as well as the results from the new tech basketball and wearables.

There was so much activity, ideas, and data that Coach Geek was getting confused on where they should focus. He was overwhelmed because these basketball coaches were throwing out ideas left and right. They all seemed to be cut from the "Ready, Fire, Aim" cloth, and Ron was not built that way. He was a steady, process-oriented guy and would often get confused by the terminology and quick actions the coaches adopted. The other coaches all seemed comfortable in that chaos and they would just jump to the latest idea and not look back at what was working from previous days. It felt like the coaches were going back to the way things were before when they tried too many ideas and were not great at anything. Ron needed to think about things a little, and build them into the plan, but the coaches just wanted to try every freakin' thing that came flying at them.

The pace was too fast for Ron and he needed a way to get his head wrapped around what they were doing, why they were doing it, and how they would know if it was working, or not. A great example was the cool techie Christmas presents.

The program spent over $3500 on that equipment and it wasn't very reliable. Some of the basketballs quit working already and he noticed that the data being captured from the wearables varied from device to device. If one guy wore two wearables, some of them would read vertical jump of 30" and the other would read 27".

Originally, the coaches and players were all stoked and the players were competing and trying to outdo each other, but when they realized the devices were not reliable, they just quit using them. Now, an expensive pile of techie junk was just sitting in the corner.

The smarter thing would have been to test a few items to see how they worked and how reliable the information was going to be. Lesson learned.

Coach Geek earned his nickname as he was an engineer at heart, and he wanted to get back to a more scientific process.

He had a vision of creating ideas, piloting them, evaluating, applying lessons learned, and if successful, rolling them out to production. Then he would continue to collect data in production to ensure they continued to add value.

Ron went back to his Agile software training, and introduced a little tool, called Trello. It allowed Bozeman's coaching staff to see all ideas and where they were in evaluating those ideas and implementing them. He tried to remember everything the coaches brought up over the past few days and used them to build the initial Trello Board.

Ron opened the daily stand-up meeting by saying, "Look guys, I'm not cut from the same cloth as you. I need some time to process and analyze things to make intelligent recommendations. I feel like we are bringing up a lot of good ideas, but we're getting lost in what's working well and what's not." Ron went on, "Honestly to me, it feels very chaotic, like we are trying too many ideas and not giving them enough time to decide if we like them or don't like them. It seems unfocused and unproductive."

Ron then displayed the newest item in their technical arsenal. "I want to show you this Trello Board where I captured all the ideas everyone brought up over the past few days," Ron had their attention. "As you can see, we have columns that show how we move these ideas from creation through to acceptance. As we come up with new ideas or fixes to existing ideas, we put them on this board and decide how we want to prioritize and focus on them. If something's not working, we can decide whether we keep trying or just scrap it. I'd like us to quickly cover this with the players. I want them to see that we make mistakes too and that we are trying to learn from them," Ron concluded.

The coaches grumbled about more technology but agreed that they were getting scattered and needed to focus. Ron felt better, but he still knew these ultra-competitive cats would need to be herded again and again! He then went into more detail about the Trello board.

Lesson 25

 Ron was able to re-focus the coaches and had a plan to better discipline their approach so they could better manage change. Change can be hard and it's easy to fall back to old ways. As you institute change in your organization, continuously assess if old behavior is returning and find creative ways (or tools) to focus your team on the path forward.

Chapter Twenty-Six: Strategy must compliment culture

This morning, Coach Geek challenged the staff to review the Trello Board and decide which are the top 3-5 areas to focus. The coaches made a list of things on their whiteboards and after much discussion and some passionate disagreement (coaches are wired this way and passionate disagreement is the norm) they agreed to disagree, but Coach Woodward would break the tie as he had the deciding vote.

Coach Woodward was impressed with Coach Geek. He was prepared, organized and held the staff accountable for every minute on their meeting agenda. And, he was bringing some balance to this coaching staff.

Coach Geek had a project manager's background and it served him well. He had Jason record every meeting so they could capture action items, define which coach was on point to drive a resolution, and ensure every action was accompanied by a deadline. They quickly learned that if they couldn't assign a deadline, the action wasn't that important. Each day they updated their progress and reported back to the rest of the coaching staff and team.

Every meeting started on time and moved quickly and with precision. Coach Woodward loved the efficiency of these meetings and decided a culture shift was needed in practice as well. He and his staff decided every practice would be two hours maximum. It was incumbent on the coaches to get results in a timely and efficient manner. The coaching staff developed three practice rules:

1. **Economy of Language**: Coach the players in 10 seconds or less speaking spurts. Be quick and

precise in your descriptions and demands. Less is more was the coaching philosophy on the court. The goal was efficient communication with little down time for the players. More activity meant more productivity and less talking meant more repetitions.

2. **Teaching Progressions Drive Progress**: The team would participate in rotational drills every day called the 'Daily Dozen' which would re-emphasize their fundamental-based skill set each day. Ball handling, shooting, rebounding, and individual and team defensive concepts were broken down into progression drills that built on and complimented each other.

3. **Player Participation is Expected**: Instead of coaches telling players what to do, coaches were expected to ask questions that forced players to articulate answers quickly and concisely. During video evaluations players were expected to coach themselves first, then help coach each other. They were trying to drive a culture of empowerment and self-improvement. Coaches were challenged to be better teachers with less negative reinforcement and to create more positive opportunities for players to take ownership of their own self-coaching process.

Woodward would be the acting CEO in practice. He roamed the floor during the Dirty Dozen, challenging coaches and players to raise their game. The CEO would insert his guidance as needed and he would time each station to ensure productive and efficient use of their practice schedule.

Jason video-taped every aspect of practice. Coach Geek watched from the top of the arena looking for ways to be more efficient from drill to drill and maximize their use of time.

Lesson 26

 Defining roles, empowering the team, reinforcing the new changes, building self-improvement awareness, and creating how management and team members communicate are critical to effectively changing the culture. It doesn't happen overnight, and you will learn and adjust along the way, but remember that your team needs continual reinforcement and encouragement to adapt.

Chapter Twenty-Seven: Danny shares

The culture was changing, and it was noticeable. Within days, players were seeing a positive difference in the coaches and their teammates. During the morning "Stand Up Meetings" as Coach Geek called them, each player had the opportunity to share their Career Best Effort (CBE) results from the previous day. These meetings were quick and pointed and they were designed for teammates to report breakthroughs that took place in their basketball or personal CBEs.

Danny Kellar volunteered to stand up one morning and shared a very personal story. He had connected by Skype with his little brother, Luke, just last night as per his CBE to call home 3x/week. He called his little brother "Squishy" as a nickname that stuck from the movie, *Finding Nemo*.

Luke needed his big brother because he was with his mom all week and she often drank too much. It was tough on the entire family and caused the marriage to split, naturally affecting both boys. With Danny away at college, Luke was on his own and it was taking a toll.

Danny shared that Luke was afraid to drive in the car with his mother. He was in tears on the phone. Danny's voice calmed him down and he allowed Luke to vent for a few minutes. Then Danny asked him a question, "Have you shared your concerns and fear with Mom?"

"No. I'm afraid to," Luke responded. Danny challenged Luke, "Which are you more afraid of, dying in a car accident or hurting Mom's feelings?"

Danny challenged Luke to wait until Mom had not been drinking but be brutally honest with her while being respectful. He told Luke to not get in the car with their

Mom unless she was sober, and he instructed Luke to call him if he ever felt pressured to get in the car with her. Luke promised to confront their mother as soon as he could.

Danny shared that he ended the call by telling his little brother, "I love you, Squishy. Never forget while I might be at school, I'm always here for you."

As he was sharing, you could have heard a pin drop. Everyone seemed to be holding their breath, feeling the pressure that Luke and Danny must be feeling, and hoping that Luke would stay safe.

Danny continued, "Luke confronted Mom late last night and called me back afterward. He said that he was nervous as hell, but at least for now she seemed to hear him and promised to stop driving while she drank." Time would tell, but at least he felt like Squishy was safe.

After Danny got done talking, you could feel a small sigh of relief. Some of the guys could relate well because they came from rough neighborhoods, broken homes, and ugly divorces. For others, his story was a real eye-opener. These guys led Brady Bunch lives in nice suburbs, and the most they ever worried about was their Saturday night date. They had never really met anyone (or at least didn't really talk to anyone) with home problems.

They're 18-22-year-old kids who didn't often share their genuine feelings. This was the first time that a teammate had the guts to share such a personal and heartfelt story and it impacted the players and coaches. Danny's courage to share seemed to crack open the floodgates a little and give his teammates the strength to share other personal stories. Over the next several Stand Up meetings, his teammates shared stories that included family matters, eating habits, playing less video games, and connecting with more people on campus. The culture of the team was changing. The personal CBE strategy was helping build a stronger bond because the players (and coaches) could see each other as real people, not just basketball players. The connectivity around sharing their successes and failures was beginning to build stronger relationships.

During the coach's meetings the CBE strategy was discussed often. Coach Woodward decided he would visit with each player and coach for 20-30 minutes every single Monday to review their CBE and discuss ways to improve moving forward. This was a huge time commitment but over time, it also became Woodward's favorite part of coaching. He felt truly connected to his players and they felt like he really loved them and cared about them.

This is how you build a team and a family, Woodward thought to himself.

Lesson 27

 Danny breaks the ice by sharing a personal challenge. This opened the door to allow other players to show their vulnerability. And, Coach Woodward realized that this was how he could really connect with his players as people. Sharing life's difficulties helps all of us understand that we are human, and it provides a genuine way to connect.

Chapter Twenty-Eight: Winning will take care of itself

Coach Woodward was pleased as the team was improving, and his coaches were focused on the right outcomes. He wondered how this culture shift would affect their wins and losses. After seven days of meetings and practices, he asked Ron Marshall to go have a beer. This was a time for basketball preparation on steroids. Now that conference games were approaching, the same pressure to win haunted Woodward.

The two new friends went to Moose's Saloon just across the town line and ordered a pitcher of amber beer and a large pizza with extra cheese. This was a classic college-town pizza joint where patrons got a bucket of peanuts and were free to throw the shells on the floor. It boasted a lot of sports history on the walls, including several of Bozeman's basketball teams.

Coach Woodward loved this place and enjoyed coming here after a big win. He'd even come here after a loss, but usually he liked to lick his wounds with a syrupy stack of pancakes at home. In three days, the conference season would begin but for now, a jock and a geek would just visit in a booth with some food, drinks, and pictures of their team all around them. They sat and chatted for a bit, not saying much of substance but enjoying each other's company.

Coach Geek liked Woodward and Woodward was fascinated by Ron Marshall's thought process.

"Coach Geek, are you having fun?" Woodward asked.

"I'm having a freaking blast!" Coach Geek shot back. "Are you?"

Woodward thought for a minute, "I'll have fun when we win."

Ron Marshall looked at Coach Woodward, thought for a moment until the silence was deafening except for, ironically, The Electric Light Orchestra playing in the background. As 'Don't Bring Me Down' played on, Coach Geek could feel his spirit getting pulled down just like the song.

"You don't get it do you, Coach Woodward?" Marshall said with a finger pointed at the head coach. Woodward looked stunned and confused. "Ron, the object of the game is to win -- we are paid to win. What answer did you want?" Woodward shot back.

"It is not about what I want, Scott! It is about the process and how we go about our business every day. It is about the players and putting them in position to be successful. In my former job, I watched a great company basically lose their way." Now Coach Geek was on a roll, "All they wanted was profits. Politics ruled and everyone played the game to cover their own selfish ass instead of working together toward common goals. Scott, do you just want to win to promote your selfish agenda and get your next job, or do you want your team to be successful both on and off the court?"

Coach Geek saw some anger in Woodward's eyes. Woodward needed a kick in the ass and Coach Geek just unloaded a size 10 ½ to Woodward's backside.

Woodward took a drink, then a deep breath, "You are right, Ron. Damn it! I needed that reminder. Thank you. It's not easy for me because I've been playing or coaching since junior high and have always focused on doing whatever we need to do to win. If I forget again, pull me back and remind me. Please." Ron nodded, "Believe me. I get it. I got sucked into the quagmire at my last company, so I might need the same from you too. We're in this together."

Just then their pizza was delivered by a tall, dark-haired woman with hazel eyes and a smile that caught Coach Woodward's eye. He had seen her before as she greeted customers at the door. Woodward heard she was the owner's daughter and had played basketball once upon a time at Bozeman Tech.

At that precise moment, a peanut came flying across the room and hit her cheek. Woodward left his seat and stood up and asked her if she was OK. Then he took a hand full of peanuts, gave her a few and they both returned fire across the bar at two friends of Coach Woodward's. Bulls eye!

"I'm, ahhhh, Scott Woodward," he stammered.

"Hi, I'm Judy," she answered with a smile.

Judy was beautiful. She was athletic, over 6'0" tall and Coach Woodward was immediately thrown off his game by her presence. He was transfixed on her eyes. Woodward shook her hand and then wrapped his free hand on top of hers. She pulled him close and whispered, "Thanks for defending my honor, Coach."

She walked away and Woodward followed her with his eyes.

"Hey, stud," Coach Geek said, "You OK, Romeo?"

"No, not really. What was that?" Woodward shot back.

"That, my friend, is an opportunity."

"Cheers!" Woodward said as he looked over his shoulder, caught Judy's eye and they both smiled.

Lesson 28

 Everyone wants to win, but if your entire focus is just on winning, your organization will become focused only on short term goals. Profitability is important, but is a short-term focus on profitability a good long-term strategy?

Chapter Twenty-Nine: Game Time – C-3PO or Bumblebee?

It was the conference opener and Bozeman Tech would take on their close rivals and one of the preseason conference favorites, Montana A&M. The Orediggers led by Coach Kelvin Keltz, had a loaded roster including 'Flyin' Ryan Vaughn.

All the Bozeman coaches had their in-game roles defined. Coach Woodward would be the CEO and make all in-game decisions including time out adjustments, substitutions and game plan implementation.

Coach Matta would record the Good Shot/Bad Shot Chart. Coach Jake focused on the defensive end and would be tracking deflections. The goal was 40 deflections per game. Coach Kevin Holly had eyes on the offense and would be charting all half court possessions by passes/possession and reversals/possession. He would evaluate how many times the ball swung from one side of the court to the other for all half-court possessions.

Coach Jason was on video evaluation and would focus on key teaching clips for the players at halftime.

Coach Geek was on point for overall quality control. He would sit in the video tower with Jason and assist in marking key possessions and produce a snapshot report on the Career Best Effort stats. These snapshots were shared with each coach during every media timeout in real time on the SharePoint app they used for practice and games.

The app measured effort/execution on defense in real time: (Note: most of the information was input by the managers who sat together behind the bench and constantly communicated with each other)

- Defensive deflections (Goal: 20/half)
- 50-50 ball retrievals for and against (Goal: 80% of all loose balls)
- % of shots challenged (Goal: 100% of all opponent's shots are met with a hand in their face)

The app would also share information around effort/execution on offense in real time:

- Good shot vs Bad shot (Goal: 100% good shots. A good shot was defined as open, balanced, and within each individual player's range, which was pre-defined by the coaches.)
- Pre-determined Rebound Routes (Goal: 80% whenever a teammate shot the ball. All five players had to be moving to spaces pre-determined by position to provide best opportunities for offensive rebounds.)
- Defensive Block-off: (Goal: Physical contact with an opponent 100% of the time for every player on every shot.)
- # of Reversals/Possession (Goal: Minimum of two reversals/ half court possession.)

The managers and coaches were all tracking their assigned stats on the connected Surface tablets, and the data was being automatically uploaded into SharePoint in real-time. Coach Geek monitored everything to make sure that all the data was flowing as expected. Coach Woodward could check his dashboard on his app whenever he wanted. It was segregated by each media time out, by half, and for the entire game. The coaching staff was organized, focused, and each role was clearly defined with expectations understood. They had practiced this several times during scrimmages, but Coach Geek was surprised about how well it was working in a live game situation.

In the first ten minutes of this first conference game, the team was trying to execute their game plan, but it was a mess. The players were trying to think about the details of their responsibilities and be as perfect as the coaches had taught in practice. They seemed almost robotic and hesitant and the Orediggers sensed their indecisiveness and pounced on the Bison early for a 20-11 lead.

Coach Woodward called a timeout.

"Guys, settle down," Woodward was calm yet direct. "Look, rely on your repetitions. Keep this simple. You all are trying to be perfect. Set a goal right now to excel in one area of our Career Best Effort Strategy. Be good at one thing and then build on that one thing. We don't want perfect robots. We want you to give your best effort. Winning will take care of itself. Trust our system, settle down and just play hard."

You could feel a collective sigh of relief as the huddle broke up. The Bison settled down and took the lead with under one minute to go in the first half, 45-42.

Halftime was a flurry of activity, and most of it was well organized, considering this was the first game coordinating all of these CBE stats and video clips. The coaching staff met outside the locker room to study the numbers. Players picked up their phones and accessed the SharePoint app to review the CBEs. Jason then fed their internal video clips to the locker room monitors. There were five key clips. The first was titled "Dysfunction" as the starting players completely broke down defensively and look confused. The second video clip showed a loose ball corralled by their opponents because that player dove for the ball while three Bison observed.

The next three clips were after Coach Woodward's timeout. One showed Bozeman Tech executing three reversals for a layup, the next a challenged shot that led to a long miss, all five Bozeman players made physical contact on their block offs which led to a run out and a dunk for Kellar! Players cheered and high fived. The last was a clip of Coach Woodward jumping up and down and ripping his pants after the dunk. The locker room erupted with laughter.

In came Woodward. "We havin' fun?"

"YES, SIR!" the team cheered as one.

"Good, keep having fun by believing in each other. Believe in our CBEs, believe in our coaches, believe in HOW WE PLAY!" Woodward shouted. "Now let's clean up a few things." Jason had three more video clips for review.

Woodward turned it into a 'Lessons Learned' meeting for the next five minutes. The players shared teaching points and positive feedback as well as constructive feedback. Everyone was engaged and eager to identify areas of failure and areas of success.

"OK, listen you guys battled hard especially after the first ten minutes when you all played more like C3PO before you figured it out and suddenly became Transformers." Woodward was having fun and the players sensed it, "We need more Bumblebees in the second half!"

Lesson 29

 Plan and delegate responsibilities based on your team's talents and leadership abilities. Promote internal leadership and don't forget to allow the members of your team and overall organization to be active participants in their own rescue. Most importantly, remember to have fun!

Chapter Thirty: EVERY DAY IN EVERY WAY WE GET A LITTLE BETTER!

The players left the locker room and did just that as Bozeman Tech trounced the Orediggers in the 2nd half. The final score was 88-72 and suddenly this 3-6 team from their non-conference slate was now 1-0 in conference play.

After the traditional handshake line, the players sprinted to the locker room. There was a different feeling as Coach Woodward opened the door to an enthusiastic celebration. Woodward stood and watched when suddenly Coach Geek came busting into the room and jumped right into the middle of the celebration. He was jumping up and down, dancing and screaming, "EVERY DAY IN EVERY WAY WE GET A LITTLE BETTER! EVERY DAY IN EVERY WAY WE GET A LITTLE BETTER! …"

It was pandemonium and Coach Geek led the madness as every player fed off his childlike celebration and geeky dance moves.

Brian Clark threw his hands up in the air and said, "Everybody, be quiet!"

He and Danny Kellar were their internal leaders, and everyone stopped and looked at their team captain.

"We have worked our asses off since Christmas and look at us. We are no longer the Bad News Bears, we are Freakin' Bison!" Clark exclaimed as players and coaches exploded in cheers. "Coach Woodward, you have taught us how to be successful and we will continue to be successful IF we stay focused on our process. This is not about one win; this is about being successful on and off the court! Coach Woodward, I once called you a fraud. I was wrong, you are the real deal!" Clark hugged his coach.

Coach Woodward then entered the circle of sweaty jerseys and smiling faces, "Gentlemen, this is not about me, this is about WE! Brian is right, I was a fraud, but I learned from my mistakes. And while winning is important, our team's success and your success in life is now my focus and our coaching staff's focus. Our collective focus is on long term success." Coach Woodward paused.

"We owe a big thanks to Coach Geek as he just defined what we are all about. We owe this to all of you who executed exactly what we wanted to execute because you believe in each other and our team. From now on after every practice and every game here is our battle cry, "EVERY DAY IN EVERY WAY WE GET A LITTLE BETTER! EVERY DAY IN EVERY WAY WE GET A LITTLE BETTER! ... HELL YES!" Woodward shouted.

By now every player and coach were jumping in unison and chanting their defining battle cry so even the fans could hear them out in the arena! Woodward's boss, Alan Johnson stood in the hallway just outside the locker room door and he heard Clark and Woodward. He heard it all. He contemplated walking in but instead walked away. The word "fraud" haunted him.

The AD had his win, but what he heard in that locker room stayed with him as he walked down the hallway still hearing Woodward's team cheer with delight.

Lesson 30

Always give credit for the win to your team, your managers, and your directors. As the leader of your organization, always take the blame for the losses, then reinforce/re-create the new positive vision for the next challenge and move on.

Chapter Thirty-One: No pancakes tonight!

The team was anything but perfect, but on this night, they learned how to believe in each other, their CBE strategy, and how to be successful TOGETHER!

Woodward and his staff would meet at Moose's! As Scott was leaving the arena, he saw a tall, young lady on the concourse, and he recognized her. "Hi, Judy!"

"Great game, Coach! Congratulations," she smiled.

"Thanks, Judy. Hey, it's a win," Coach Woodward responded with his own big smile.

"I heard you played here. You were an All-American, weren't you?" asked Woodward.

"How did you know? You stalking my Facebook page?" Judy's hazel eyes lit up.

"You caught me. Care to join us for a beer?" Scott shyly asked as his coaches came barreling in through the door behind him.

"I thought you'd never ask," she chuckled lightly. They both laughed. Coach thought, *No pancakes tonight. Time to celebrate!*

Lesson 31

 Celebrate your victories with the people you love!

Chapter Thirty-Two: Block or charge? You need to have a sense of humor.

Travel is brutal in the northern inter-mountain Rockies in January and February. It's dark and icy, and the bus rides are long and rough.

Even though the weather was merciless, these Bison were getting better. This was not an opinion. It was a verifiable fact and the data showed it. On this late January night, however, Coach Woodward was miserable as he sat in the front seat of the bus headed home from a gut-wrenching loss at Great Falls University. It had come down to a shoot-out. Bozeman had a shot to win at the buzzer, but it rimmed out and they lost 85-84.

Great Falls was a conference contender and road wins against top teams in the Frontier Conference are hard to come by. Tonight, was a disappointing loss.

Woodward watched as the white snow-packed road rolled beneath him and as the northern lights showed brightly through his frost-edged window. He replayed every call and every play in his head. These losses stung.

Coach Geek walked up the bus aisleway and asked, "Coach, you mind if I sit down?"

"Sure, what's up Ron?" Woodward asked.

"Coach, I know you are down, but we are getting better. Look at this!" Ron exclaimed.

Coach Geek pulled up his app and showed the game trends from their Career Best Effort Stats. "Look at deflections, % of offensive rebounds, % of physical block offs on each shot, close out success rate, % of challenged shots..."

"I know, but we didn't win," Woodward responded.

Ron looked disappointedly at Woodward and paused to gather his words, "Listen. We talked about this before. Either you believe in our process and recognize our improvement, or you don't."

"Here, please review this, Coach. I know you are disappointed, but let's talk when you are ready," Ron said in a hushed dejected tone.

One thing about Coach Geek, he ain't scared, Woodward thought to himself. Woodward also knew Coach Geek was right.

Woodward picked up the computer and checked out all the numbers. Almost every CBE stat was up 10% or better for the team. On top of that, every player since Christmas had markedly improved their productivity in the desired areas.

Coach Woodward knew every team member was looking to him for leadership. He stood up, had the driver turn on the overhead lights, and asked for everyone's attention and paused while they turned off their video games and stopped the movie on the overhead screens.

"We are all disappointed in this result tonight. Yes, we had our chances, but it wasn't about the last shot. It was about our execution or lack thereof." Woodward continued, "Guys, Coach Geek just handed me a review of our CBE stats and we are getting better, a lot better! We got hammered at Great Falls last season by 30. Tonight, we lost by one measly point."

"Here is what I want you to know. Our culture changed. Heck, everything changed one month ago. We all have changed for the better, on and off the court. Do you agree?" Everyone answered, "Yes, sir" in unison.

"We are not championship caliber yet but with continued concentration and effort every day in every way we get a little better, right? How much better can Great Falls get?" he asked but wanted no reply.

"I don't know about Great Falls, but I could make the argument we are the most improved team in the country since our 0-3 start. I believe we also have the highest ceiling to improve in our conference." The players clapped at this.

Coach put his hands up to stop the clapping. "Don't be satisfied with close. Don't be satisfied, period. We are on a journey of continuous improvement and that journey never ends. Are you all willing to take that journey together and see how far we can go?"

"YES, SIR!" was the resounding answer reverberating off the bus walls.

Coach Woodward winked at Ron Marshall.

Just then a rabbit ran in front of the bus and the driver swerved a bit to miss it. Coach Woodward stumbled and grabbed hold of the seat beside him to keep from falling, then everyone heard the thud. That rabbit was flattened! "What was that," asked Woodward, and the bus driver looked over his shoulder and responded calmly with one word, "Rabbit."

"Was that a block or a charge Coach Woodward?" Coach Geek asked.

The bus erupted in gallows laughter.

Lesson 32

 Fight the urge for immediate gratification. Sometimes progress is hidden. You must become aware of the data and trust the data. Also, a sense of humor can go a long way.

Chapter Thirty-Three: A leader begins to face his demons

February flew by and this team that started 3-6 in non-conference play and was the pre-season pick for 8th place, was now 9-6 and tied for 4th place. There were three games remaining in conference play. The Bison were 12-12 overall, but for Coach Woodward, 17 consecutive losing seasons still felt like an anvil weighing on him. Going .500 or better was within reach, and the team was focused and excited for the stretch run.

Coach Woodward had changed. They had all changed. While winning was always the anticipated result, it was more about the players and the process. The players were also doing better academically; their mid-term grades were up, and their 3.2 GPA goal was well within sight!

Alan Johnson, the athletic director, was still Alan Johnson but even he seemed at least interested in what the team was doing both on and off the floor.

Their AD/coach relationship was based on mutual tolerance when crossing each other's path. They both agreed to tolerate the other's faults, so long as Woodward won games. On this morning after a road trip loss to Denver, Johnson asked for a meeting with his coach in his office. Johnson never set foot in Woodward's office just to visit. It was always on Johnson's turf and during the season, they only met after a loss.

"Coach, have a seat." Johnson motioned to the small seat in front of his desk. Woodward noticed he was sitting lower than Johnson and tried to sit up a little taller to make things more even. He wanted to feel like he was on the same level.

"Scott, I am interested in all this talk about metrics and methodology and process. What are you doing?" Alan asked.

Woodward responded, "We decided just before Christmas we needed to re-evaluate our path forward. We felt we were making some progress, but we were trying too many things and we also felt we needed to change our culture." Woodward leaned forward and continued, "Our team needed to be more focused on successful behaviors and less focused on the end results of wins and losses."

"Wait a minute, Coach," his boss interrupted. "Winning is how you are evaluated. You understand that, right?"

"You have every right to evaluate me however you want, but I have the right to run my team as I see fit as long as I am the head coach," Woodward responded calmly. "My contract with my players is more diverse and layered than simple metrics around winning and losing. We believe consistent practice and reinforcement of the right behaviors drive positive results. We believe in building internal leadership and self-coaching. We decided to invest in each other by recognizing individual progress based on a Career Best Effort system we have developed for each player and coach."

"What is a Career Best Effort?" Alan leaned forward and seemed surprisingly interested.

"Career Best Effort is a strategy that is personally driven. It allows players and coaches to establish their own expectations and identify individual actions that take no specific talent but do require concentration and effort. In fact, I have Danny Kellar's weekly CBE results right here. I just met with him to reinforce his CBE activities," Woodward explained.

Alan Johnson scanned the CBE, then looked at Woodward, "Interesting." Johnson looked out the window and then back at Coach Woodward.

"Scott, you must continue to make significant progress to keep your job. A conference title would certainly assure a new contract, but I have to say I like what I am seeing. I appreciate the progress you have made. For me, it is still primarily about winning and now is the time to win," Johnson paused.

"Any consideration for our players' academic improvement?" Coach Woodward asked. "Any consideration for how much our team has improved and how our players have committed to excellence both on and off the court?"

"Scott, I'm not going to promise anything, but I will give it some consideration. I do see the team's progress," Johnson responded.

"Is there anything else I can answer for you, Alan?" Coach Woodward asked politely. "No, not right now," Alan responded.

As Alan Johnson watched his coach walk out the door, he pulled out a pen and paper and began to scratch down some bullets.

- *What would my Career Best Effort look like?*
  - o *Meet with my head coaches weekly*
  - o *Attend a weekly practice to see how they are run*
  - o *Attend all home games for every sport whenever possible*

o *At the end of each season, meet with each
coach to understand what they need for
success*
o *Establish an athletic department Vision,
Mission, and Values*
o *Personal*

■ *Hmmm*

Johnson had demons from his past and was starting to realize they interfered with his ability to connect with his coaches and lead his department. He was intrigued by this team and their new way of working, and he wanted to learn more.

Lesson 33

Bad leaders can change, too, IF they can set aside their egos, IF they open their minds, IF they open their hearts, and IF they face their demons.

Chapter Thirty-Four: Every teams needs a Junk Yard Dog!

3:00PM. Practice time.

Players bounced around in their pre-practice routine. The staff had devised a quick-paced pre-practice routine that took 12 minutes each day. There were six different two-minute drills and the results were posted each day on the locker room monitors and in SharePoint. Each player would check their progress, and it might have generated a bit of healthy competitive peer pressure.

These drills were high-spirited and set the tone for the rest of the practice. All coaches were engaged, energetic, positive, and assisted in recording results. Negative reinforcement did happen on occasion but typically only when a player exhibited a lack of concentration and/or effort. It was not personal but was enforced directly and swiftly. It was quick and simple, and players were soon rewarded with another chance to get it right and then praised when they did, in fact, get it right.

Practice was a teaching progression where every drill was related, and each fundamental was built on top of the other. Woodward was a great teacher and he helped his assistants grow as teachers by coaching them in his daily coaches-only Stand-up Meeting.

Because Coach Geek was monitoring the data from every drill, during water breaks, he would often recognize who had posted the best scores in the two-minute drills. He posted this on the TV monitors in the gym and the players loved it! Every one-minute water break was more than a break, it was a time to reward great effort, quality and productivity. It could also be a time for constructive criticism where needed.

Practices were competitive, and there were winners and losers in every drill and scrimmage situation. The players told the coaches they wanted to compete, and the practices were full of competition. While each player knew the importance of executing successful behavior, they also wanted to be trained on competing while executing those fundamental tasks. Winners high-fived and losers did 10 push-ups. Coach Geek tracked who won and lost every single day in every single drill. The players loved it!

He and Jason created the Junk Yard Dog award from an action hero doll of the old wrestler, Sylvester Ritter (aka, the Junk Yard Dog.) The Junk Yard Dog was given out after each practice to the player whose defensive hustle was relentless. It was a coveted award that brought serious bragging rights and the winner proudly displayed the doll on his locker for the day. The player who earned it the most during the season would be added to the JYD plaque, which hung in the locker room.

Players believed in practicing with precision. They had a collective focus on productivity, and they all believed success would follow. The new system was working!

Lesson 34

 Productivity is the result of a good fundamental base, reinforced by focused and efficient teachers/leaders. Everyone must be committed and demand perfection from each other as a team. Quality is not negotiable.

Chapter Thirty-Five: Can you be a great coach and have a losing record?

Coach Woodward was seeing progress. The players were executing better and were more focused. His assistants were focused and clear about their roles and goals. Woodward was excited about the prospects of the team coming down the stretch and because of their collective improvements as a staff and as players, Woodward felt his team could contend for the conference title. That was a long way from their 0-3 start!

He still felt the pressure of winning, but he was learning to be at peace with the results and was proud of the program they were building.

Coach Geek was doing amazing work. He had driven the cultural change to one of complete accountability, focused on quality and had sold the players and coaches on individual, and collective productivity and continuous improvement. As a result, the coaches and team were all growing in confidence.

Coach Woodward was gearing up for the stretch run and called for a coach's meeting at his home. He wanted the meeting to be relaxed but he still had a clear agenda. Before the meeting started, there was the usual banter among friends who competed hard and partied hard.

Coach Woodward loved his staff and they were his family. Balance in life wasn't his best talent but he was getting better. He and Judy had been spending a lot of time with each other and it helped him see that there was more to life than basketball. He had created his own Career Best Effort Strategy both professionally and personally. He held himself accountable everyday as follows:

I call Judy every day and tell her how much she means to me	(1) (2) (3) (4) (5) (6) (7)
I meet with each player and coach every Monday for a minimum of 20 minutes and keep notes from each meeting	He listed each of their names
I exercise 5x/week for better health	(1) (2) (3) (4) (5)
I do not snack after 7PM (except for after wins 😊)	(1) (2) (3) (4) (5) (6) (7)
I attend one campus event/week outside of athletics	(1)
I support my colleagues by dropping in at other sport practices or attending other team's games or other organization's events on campus 2x/week	(1) (2)

This informal coaches' meeting was one part of that strategy to better connect with his coaching staff each month. It was their bonding time, and time for Woodward to ask questions, get input, and have fun away from the office.

Once the banter subsided, Woodward spoke up, "Can you be a successful coach and have a losing record?"

Silence came across the room. Ron Marshall just smiled at Coach Woodward. Woodward already knew where Coach Geek stood on this issue.

Jason thought about it for ten silent seconds, had an initial reaction, and said it out loud, "Is success winning or developing quality personal relationships?"

Coach Donnie Matta said, "Winning. We are paid to win."

The old veteran, Coach Porter "Jake" Jacobsen, responded immediately, "I got into coaching to make a difference. Yes, I want to win but I love to teach, mentor, make a difference in young men's lives. I've been hired and fired, and I have learned to never fear being fired. I learned that the relationships you build are the lasting reward of coaching, not the wins and losses."

Matta nodded his head and reflected on that answer. Coach Matta had played at Kentucky, Big Blue Nation, where winning was everything. He was a Division 1 animal who was hyper competitive. He respected Coach Jake a lot and he always wondered why the players loved Jake so much. Now he knew.

Coach Woodward then spoke up, "Professionally, it states right in my contract that winning is important and I, no we, will be evaluated on wins and losses. There are some other areas mentioned around academic performance, etc. but we all know the reality of this business."

"It's not fair to be evaluated only on wins!" said Coach Matta.

Woodward responded in a thoughtful and measured tone, "Donnie, you're funny. You just said a coach is not successful unless they win."

"Yeah but…," Matta stopped. He knew he was wrong.

Coach Woodward looked every man in the eye and said, "Look, we are in this together. We have three conference games left and then the conference tournament. Are we going to become frauds like I was earlier in the year, breaking our huddles with '1-2-3 WIN!' Or, are we going to continue to build a culture of WE? Are we willing to trust our process and break old selfish habits? Are we willing to battle down the stretch for each other? Are we willing to stay true to our new culture both on and off the court, and create even better bonds with our players?"

The answers to all of Woodward's questions were clear. While winning is important, investing in the player's lives and learning from team lessons that would become life lessons would be their focus. Their collective measure of success now, and moving forward, would not be winning or losing. The wins and losses would take care of themselves. Now the coaching staff and players would need to trust each other, trust their process and either win or lose, TOGETHER!

Lesson 35

Real coaching is caring about the people in your organization. Next, it is about challenging your team and your organization to be the best they can be. While you want your leaders striving to win, every now and then they need to be reminded of why they coach. Their role is not to blame their colleagues or team when a project goes south. Instead, their role is to create an atmosphere where a team and their leaders can make mistakes, learn from their mistakes, hopefully self-correct, and apply lessons learned to avoid repeating the same mistakes.

Chapter Thirty-Six: Honesty

Coach Woodward opened practice differently on this day than he had on any other day. There would be no opening Daily Dozen. He knew his players were aware of the questions that were floating across campus regarding his job status. Alan Johnson had hung him out in the wind by leaking the late season expectations to the media a few weeks ago, even before their most recent meeting. An unnamed source had a name and Woodward knew it was his boss.

"Toes on the baseline men. Eyes on me," Woodward ordered. As Coach Woodward began to walk down the line of men, every player locked their eyes on him.

Just then Alan Johnson opened the door and walked into the practice gym. He was quiet and stood back. He just wanted to blend in, and watch Coach Woodward speak to his team.

Woodward never saw Alan enter on the opposite side of the gym. "You guys are my family and real families don't hide challenges," he began. "You all have taught me coaching is much more than winning. My contract clearly states winning is important and I will certainly be evaluated by wins and losses."

He continued, "You all have heard the rumors about my future at Bozeman Tech. You probably read the story online recently suggesting our team needs to make the playoffs and then win the conference championship for me to keep my job." Woodward looked at every player as he paused.

"The words 'Me' and 'My' no longer fit our basketball family," Woodward said. "WE have each other, and that is far more important. I have learned that a culture of WE will defeat the disease of ME every damn time," Woodward stated as a matter of fact.

"We need to get a few things straight before tomorrow night's game." Woodward stood silent for a few seconds with his hands behind his back. Then he spoke in a steady and measured cadence, "Can we guarantee we all will give our Career Best Effort today and every day until our season is over? Can we be loyal to each other? Can we stay focused on the right things and not let outside distractions like today's article tear us apart? I'm asking you?"

One by one Coach Woodward walked down the line of players with their toes on the baseline. One by one, each player gave him a "Yes, sir" with conviction. Every assistant coach followed suit.

The team could feel the weight of the final week of the season upon them, but also excited about how far they had come. Woodward had one more thing to say, "Now let's have fun by playing hard and executing TOGETHER as a family."

Then the two team leaders, Danny Kellar and Brian Clark, approached their coach. The rest of the players followed suit and surrounded him holding hands. Woodward stood in the middle. They all walked forward and closed ranks with hands touching above his head. They started chanting, "EVERY DAY IN EVERY WAY WE GET A LITTLE BETTER! EVERY DAY IN EVERY WAY WE GET A LITTLE BETTER! …", and they got louder and before long, their chant was echoing all around the gym and throughout the building.

Alan Johnson left the gym, unseen by the team. He walked down the hallway and stopped for a moment. He took a deep breath to gather his thoughts around what he had just witnessed. He was glad he heard that moment of honesty, and he was glad he saw and heard the player's responses. Johnson was starting to understand how this team was evolving, and maybe he could learn from them.

The next seven days were full of drama in the media around the rumors and conjecture on the future of Coach Scott Woodward.

This team was impervious to it all. They were too focused to let any outside nonsense effect their practices. Kellar and Clark were junk yard dogs and leading their pack on a mission.

Lesson 36

The more a leader avoids the elephant in the room, the more the leader becomes a lesser leader. You must talk about the hard stuff. The world isn't always easy, and your people know that. Teach them how to handle adversity. Your team will learn from your example, you'll build more respect, and you'll build a tighter team bond.

Chapter Thirty-Seven: Bozeman Rolls!

Bozeman Tech was playing their best basketball of the season and their defense was stifling. They swept into Salt Lake City and beat Eastern Utah 67-63. The coaching staff was now clicking, and their data gathering and analysis were improving with each passing game. Woodward felt his staff and their ability to evaluate real-time data and trends was becoming a competitive advantage.

Bozeman's process was smooth as silk by now. Media timeouts were well-planned and timed. Coach Woodward huddled with Coach Jake away from the team for an update on what was working and where he saw a need for adjustments. The rest of the staff shared specific statistical updates with the players around offensive and defensive efficiency stats to better gauge the success or challenges to their game plan. Each coach had :10 sec or less to share their most important piece of information.

This would take :20-:30 seconds, then players had whatever time was left to interact and react to the information prior to Coach Woodward joining the huddle. Player comments were to be positive and reinforce teaching points made by the coaches. Kellar and Clark were on point to monitor and lead that segment with the players in the huddle. Then Coach Woodward would address the team with strategic points for the next possession or make any other needed adjustments.

All of this was under the watchful eyes of the managers who timed each segment and recorded the dialogue for post-game review. Coaches and players would review game timeouts in team video review typically the following day. This was most instructive and allowed everyone to critique their own performance during timeouts. Even players not in the game were evaluated for their input and engagement.

It also provided a review of who listened well and executed what Coach Woodward prescribed coming out of every timeout. Coach Woodward and the supporting stat updates from assistant coaches were also on tape to evaluate their economy of language and delivery of their coaching points.

Woodward constantly reminded his team to stay focused on the process. Momentum was on their side and one thing Woodward had learned is to not rock the boat when things were going well. You can sink the boat and rebuild it as they did earlier in the season but now this team was on a roll.

The next two games confirmed the coach's gut feel about this team. The Bison had now won three in a row. They were now 15-12 and clinched fourth place and finished 12-6 in conference play. They made the conference playoffs!!

In the Frontier Conference semi-finals, they dominated the conference regular season champions, Sioux Falls University, on the road, 75-55. The number two seed, Great Falls, won at home versus Montana A&M.

The perennial losers from Bozeman would now travel to Great Falls to play for the Frontier Conference Championship in one week. A win there would then take them to an NCAA tournament bid on ESPN! That was the 'WHAT', but the team needed to stay focused on 'WHY' they were so much more successful than earlier in the season. The answer was simple. The team was locked in and true to their team strategy and individual CBE strategies. When everyone on the team committed to getting a little bit better every day, the results followed.

One more game!

Lesson 37

Coach Woodward realized his team was not only getting better, but every team goal was now in sight. Trust the process was his mantra. After all, the changes, and repetitions of what was important had the team believing in and supporting each other.

Chapter Thirty-Eight: Some friendly advice from an ESPN national college basketball analyst

Forty-Five minutes before game time is the worst time for any head basketball coach. The locker room is empty except for the pre-game radio interview. Then there comes the ten-minute stretch when the head coach is all alone. It is quiet, it is painfully quiet except for the sound of the pep bands playing in the gym seeping through the brick walls.

Coach Woodward was alone with his thoughts. He remembered his first day when he arrived on campus three years ago. The program was in disarray; the players lacked commitment and were basically just floating rudderless down the river.

Back then, no one cared. Now, it was different. His players were different. His coaches were different, and he was different. That last week of practices were just as gritty as the rest. His team hustled, dove after loose balls, and played relentless physical defense. They continued striving to improve their personal CBEs and they challenged each other to work their butts off. They stayed true to the course they set way back at Christmas.

Tonight, his team would play on national TV in front of a packed house with an NCAA tournament bid on the line. He knew they had to win this game for him to keep his job, but he compartmentalized that haunting thought and instead focused on how grateful he was for his team, for his coaches, and for this opportunity.

He thought of Judy and how she helped him gain balance and made him feel whole again. She was guiding him to become a better person each day. He was no longer a fraud who put winning above all else. He was focused on improving as a person, helping his players become more accountable, better teammates and productive members to their basketball family and the campus community. ESPN's Mark Adams dropped in on Coach Woodward. Adams was known as the 'Voice of the Mid-Majors.' He and Woodward were friends from coaching and Adams had broadcast many Bozeman Tech games in the last three seasons. Adams had seen this coach and this program rise from the dead and he was a huge fan!

"Coach Woodward, I had to drop by and wish you all my best tonight," Adams said with a smile. "So, here's the deal, you really want to come see me after the game."

Adams explained he would interview the championship coach live on ESPN right after the final buzzer.

"Coach, can I give you some advice?" Adams asked. Woodward nodded.

"I know they will try to drag you over to me when you win tonight. Take your time, enjoy the moment, reflect on what you have done here ... I can wait for you." Woodward and Adams hugged, then he was all alone again and his thoughts turned back to his team.

Lesson 38

Under the pressure, remember to take a breath. Enjoy the moment even when you don't have time. While you will give your organization all the credit, don't be shy about taking a moment for yourself to appreciate your team's success.

Chapter Thirty-Nine: Preparing for the possibility

Woodward thought about how this group of people had truly become family. As the players clapped while jogging to the locker room awaiting their final instructions, he took a deep breath. He stood at the door and high-fived every player and coach. Players hot-footed it to the restroom for one last stop before heading back out to the court. It was quiet now as each player took a seat. Woodward paced back and forth with his head down.

"Gentlemen, in 1944 Coach John McLendon coached the North Carolina College for Negroes to a 26-1 record," *Woodward started.*

"This was Durham, NC and Jim Crow laws ruled the south as blacks and whites were not permitted to congregate, socialize or participate in athletic events. The Duke Medical School, an all-white school, was 27-0 as they barn-stormed the south but playing McLendon's team would never happen. If they did play against each other, the black players and coaches could be lynched."
Woodward then pulled out an article and read aloud:

The North Carolina College for Negroes Eagles were coming off their most successful season. John B. McLendon had just led his team to a one-loss season. Aubrey Stanley, Henry (Big Dog) Thomas, Floyd (Cootie) Brown and James (Boogie-Woogie) Hardy were the stars on a team that ran the fast break with great precision.

"We could have beaten anyone," said McClendon, who eventually became a member of the Basketball Hall of Fame. Even with their gaudy record and success, McLendon was frustrated that his team was not eligible for

participation in the National Invitational Tournament or the N.C.A.A. tournament simply because they were African Americans.

A Duke player named Jack Burgess and others attended a meeting at the local YMCA in Durham, NC where students from both sides of the tracks would meet secretly to discuss ways to overcome racism. During one of those meetings, the conversation turned to basketball and a bold challenge was issued. What about a secret game between the Eagles and the Duke Medical School teams?

John McLendon supported the clandestine game as he was curious about how his team would fair, but more importantly, he was a visionary who wanted to, "prepare my team for the possibilities someday of integration."

At Duke, there was trepidation among the team. Jack Burgess wanted to play the game, but some of his team members weren't so sure. Finally, the team came to a competitive conclusion, "We thought we could whup 'em," Duke's David Hubbell said in an earlier interview. "So, we decided to find out."

On Sunday morning March 12, 1944 just after 11:00AM, all of the Durham, NC citizens were attending church but not the Duke Medical School team members. They were driving across town toward a tiny gym on a campus that might only be a few miles away from the Duke campus but, for all intents and purposes, might as well be in another country. Affluent Duke was a place for whites only vs. McLendon's team which was all black.

"To keep from being followed, we took this winding route through town," Hubbell recalled. To avoid detection, they pulled their jackets up over their heads as they arrived

on campus and this band of white basketball players snuck into the gym.

"I had never played basketball against a white person before, and I was a little shaky," Aubrey Stanley recalled. "You did not know what might happen if there was a hard foul, or if a fight broke out. I kept looking over at Big Dog and Boogie to see what to do. They were both from up North."

"On that particular morning, you didn't exactly need to play skins and shirts," one player recalled.

They began to play, and the Duke Medical School got off to an early lead. There was a lot of nervousness on both sides but after several minutes, the Eagles realized that these white players from Duke were not invincible. The Eagles realized that they could not only play with these white men but maybe even beat them.

"About midway through the first half," Stanley says, "I suddenly realized: 'Hey, we can beat these guys. They aren't supermen. They're just men like us.'"

"They just beat the heck out of us. They were very, very good," Duke's Jack Burgess said.

The Duke players had never seen anything like this in their barnstorming games across the south. By the end of the game, the scoreboard told the entire story: Eagles 88, Duke 44.

After the two teams took a break following this history-making contest, they came together and visited. They decided to play some more ... but this time the teams would be mixed. Two or three black guys matched up with two or three white guys and they played together. They had fun and new friendships were born.

After the game, Coach McLendon called the teams together and they made a pact to never speak of this game for fear of lynching and repercussions from the law or any other Jim Crow activists in Durham at that time.

The Durham authorities were never tipped off and the community as a whole left church that morning and, for the most part, never knew of this game. There was no score sheet, no stats, and no record, just memories of a game held tightly by a coach and players from different backgrounds.

Woodward looked up from the paper and saw every set of eyes fixated as they hung on every word.

"Coach McLendon said he was, 'preparing his team for the possibilities of integration in 1944!'" Woodward shouted. "There was NO POSSIBILITY of integration in 1944 in the south," Coach Woodward emphasized, "NO POSSIBILITY!"

Then he said one word, "Preparation."

"Think about the courage it took to prepare in that way in those times when just the thought of a game like that being played could end lives," Woodward said in a soft voice.

"Gentlemen, this opportunity we embrace tonight is not pressure. In fact, that game in 1944 will forever tower over this game tonight and every other game we have ever played. But, the lesson Coach McLendon shares with us tonight is around the profound value of PREPARING well!" Woodward emphasized.

"Everything we have done since Christmas with Coach Geek and every coach and every player in this room has prepared all of us for this one moment in time. NOW … IS … YOUR … TIME!" Woodward bellowed.

The locker room exploded in cheers! GAME TIME!!!

Lesson 39

Prepare yourself for the possibilities. Dream big, you never know when, where, or how opportunity will knock. It may take days or years, but if you constantly prepare for the possibilities of success, the day opportunity knocks, you will be ready!

Chapter Forty: The evolution of halftime and timeouts

The Bison and the Great Falls Ring Necks (a ring neck is a pheasant, by the way) were both nervous early in the championship game. The bright lights of an ESPN national broadcast were not the norm in this league and both teams were tight.

During the first TV timeout, Woodward reviewed the early game trends tracked by the staff. One trend stood out and that was the collective heart rates of the starters. They were obviously stressed, and Coach Woodward stepped into the huddle, "Hey guys, remember the old movie *Dumb and Dumber?*"

All the players looked up and nodded with confused looks.

"Remember when Lloyd kept trying to ask Mary Swanson for a date and he kept putting it off, and eventually his best friend Harry got the date with Mary?" Woodward paused as every player started to smile waiting for the payoff. "Be HARRY! Don't play scared. We have nothing to lose here. Let's have some fun!"

Coach Woodward then instructed the team, "Swanson on 3!" The team broke their huddle with a, "1-2-3 Swanson!", while laughing their collective butts off!

ESPN caught it all on camera and Mark Adams was actually in the huddle listening. When he came back to the broadcast booth, they played the timeout huddle and Adams described the scene inside that huddle along with the Swanson chant. "Next thing will be Coach Woodward in a powder blue tuxedo," he quipped.

The Bison played loose and free. They spaced the floor, moved the ball, and started getting their offensive mojo. Defensively they were disciplined and active, disrupting the Great Falls offense. Bison – 25, Ring Necks – 18 with under five minutes to go in the first half. Time out Great Falls!

The last five minutes of the half became a high-level chess match. Great Falls chipped away one possession at a time and closed the gap to 35-33 at the half.

Bozeman Tech had their halftime process mastered. Jason uploaded the video clips to SharePoint. Coach Jake added game notes of specific player coaching points from the first half. One key example was Great Falls consistently adjusted to Bozeman Tech overplaying the point-to-wing reversal passes, and the Ring Necks utilized back cuts for three easy baskets in the half. Coach Jake made the adjustment to not deny the offensive players outside shoulder but rotate lower to the inside shoulder for better positioning versus the back cuts. Jason had video clips and slow motioned one play and froze the video to show Coach Jake's point.

The coaching staff had evolved from early in the season where each coach had individual responsibilities to track, to now working together in real time to bring game adjustment information to Coach Woodward and the team.

The locker room was a flurry of player activity with video review and Coach Jake's adjustment notes. The players watched while Kellar and Clark served as meeting facilitators prior to Coach Woodward's arrival at halftime. Managers video-taped the player locker room halftime meetings and two assistant coaches were assigned to observe the interactions and only engage if any comments were out of bounds or to refocus the conversation as needed.

Athletic Director, Alan Johnson even snuck into the tunnel just outside the visiting locker room where the coaches were meeting. He could hear the players coaching each other just inside the locker room door. He watched the coaches execute their halftime process with interest. Alan even gave Coach Woodward a thumbs up just before Woodward entered the locker room.

Coach Woodward walked into the locker room and was prepared as usual. He reinforced defending their back cuts and quickly reviewed their block off percentage, as rebounds in the 2nd half would be huge.

The team seemed like they were getting a little tight again, and if nothing else, he wanted them to play Bison basketball against these Ring Necks from Great Falls in the 2nd half.

"I used to have a black lab named Bandit. She was a hell of a hunting dog." Every player knew this would be good. "So, one day when she was just a pup and had never retrieved a pheasant in her life, I banged a huge ring neck and she tore off like a bat out of hell to retrieve that cock. She got to him and he wasn't dead yet but that didn't stop her. She grabbed that dude and dragged him a good 100 yards. That bird spurred her in the mouth, and she was bleeding until I walked up on the two of them basically wrestling in the dirt. I grabbed that bird looked him in the eye and wrung his neck!" Woodward stopped and looked half crazed as every player and coach looked on in amusement and a hint of laughter.

"Bandit went on to live a happy and healthy life for the next 15 years."

"The second half is about who will be the pheasant and who will be the retriever."

Just then, Coach Geek started barking and the team howled with laughter!

"Now go bag a bird!" Woodward yelled

Lesson 40

As an agile organization Woodward and his team tried creative ways to manage timeouts and halftime. Some ideas worked but others did not. Their agile process among cross functional teams of coaches and players eventually led to a highly organized and coordinated approach. It became a competitive advantage. So did Woodward's off the wall stories. It helped relax his team and make it fun. When you see your team working hard and getting tight, adding in some humor can quickly relieve the pressure.

Chapter Forty-One: The last shot

The second half was back and forth, with each team going up by as much as 4 points before the other team came charging back. The fans were going crazy! At one point, the pep band leader tore off his shirt during an attempted foul shot by the Ring Necks.

It was intense – as intense as Coach Woodward had ever witnessed. The game was on the line. The Bison had one shot to win. They had battled back from a seven-point deficit with 1:30 to go and now through a forced turnover and a couple of banged three balls they were down 75-73 with :07 seconds to go. "TIMEOUT!"

Bozeman Tech had forced another turnover on the opposite baseline and so the Bison would need to advance the ball up the court and get a good shot off in :07 seconds. That was plenty of time.

Woodward took a deep breath and entered the huddle immediately because he knew exactly the play he would use. His team had run this play hundreds of times during practice as they prepared for all late game situations. Woodward drew up the play for his leader, Brian Clark. Clark was a 37% threat from behind the arc, which was second on the team, but his heart rate under pressure was far superior than any other player they tracked throughout the season. Every game and every practice, players were put in stressful situations and Coach Geek tracked heart rates just for this moment.

"Listen to me," Woodward started. "Look over my shoulder up top in the arena. What do you see?"

The players all looked up and saw an ESPN TV camera.

"We are going to run a screen play for Clark. We will run it for our sideline. You know why?" Woodward asked. Players looked at him with a confused expression.

"Here's why. That camera will be pointing right at our bench when Brian hits this shot, and I want that ESPN camera to see us all dancing when that shot goes down! No overtime for us, we are going for it now!"

The players broke the huddle and Danny Kellar brought the five Bison teammates on the floor together. He said, "One shot, we all have our role. Brian let it fly with confidence, let's do this together!"

As the ball advanced to the front court, Clark screened for the point guard and simultaneously Kellar back screened for Clark to fade to the wing closest to the Bozeman Tech bench. He set his feet as he caught the perfect pass in his shooting pocket.

ESPN showed Clark in perfect rhythm and Coach Woodward was in the shot behind him with one fist already up. Woodward was acting as if the shot was already down! The play was executed to perfection and caught Great Falls ill-prepared.

Clark let it fly with confidence, the way Danny Kellar described just a few moments ago. Woodward raised his other fist in the air as he saw the shot was in rhythm and on target. The buzzer sounded in mid-flight. The ball rattled the rim for what seemed like an eternity and then gently rolled off and onto the floor.

Game over. Great Falls 75 Bozeman Tech 73.

Clark collapsed to the floor. Woodward ran to his player and picked him up. Every player and coach followed their head coach.

"Brian, throughout this whole season, you taught me what is really important. I am so very proud of you. You wanted the ball and you shot it with confidence," Woodward shouted as Great Falls celebrated. "We have learned how to be successful together and YOU taught me that. I am grateful you are my player!"

Brian Clark missed one shot and, yes, that one shot could have won the game and even saved his coach's job. But now, here stood his coach with tears running down his face telling him how much he loved him and how proud he was to share this one moment with him. In all the confusion of the moment, Clark remembered the day Coach Woodward looked through his office window and gave him a thumbs up as if to say, 'keep working hard son, you will be rewarded.' Little did he know, Woodward had just been informed by Jason that Clark thought his coach was a fraud.

Clark was rewarded for his honesty on this day with the loyalty and confidence from a man he had grown to love and admire.

The team lost the game, and then this bunch of interwoven success stories retreated to their locker room for one last time together with Coach Woodward.

Lesson 41

This chapter partially recounts my (Mark's) final few minutes as a head college basketball coach. I will never forget it. My player shot it with confidence, and I love him to this day. I never regretted my decision to go for the win. When your team is challenged with intense pressure, and the game is on the line, it's the relationships that you build, and the confidence you instill in your team that will make the memories.

Chapter Forty-Two: Redemption and acceptance

Coach Woodward stood in the hallway, alone. It might be the last time he would address his team as their head coach. Alan Johnson walked around the corner. He saw a man who had given his all, and he just witnessed a team which had done the same.

"Coach, I need to ask you for a favor," Alan confided. "I'd like to talk to the team before you speak. I have some things I need to say, and I need you to hear them."

Woodward looked at his boss and nodded his head. What choice did he have? Alan Johnson was still his boss.

The athletic director and the coach entered the locker room together. Alan Johnson took a deep breath and looked at Coach Woodward. "Hey guys, I wanted to come in and take just a few minutes of your time to say a few words. I grew up in a dysfunctional family where we didn't talk about our feelings. We swept our challenges under the rug," Johnson explained. "My father wasn't very understanding when I lost games as a young player. He took out his frustrations on me regardless of how I played. I never understood it, but one thing I learned was, you sure as hell better win or get your ass kicked." Johnson shook his head in disgust.

"You all have taught me coaching and playing is much more than winning. However, for me it was still all about winning, until I heard you guys after your home win to open conference play. I stood outside your locker room door and Brian Clark, I heard you. I heard you loud and clear. You said, "Coach Woodward, you have taught us how to be successful and we will continue to be successful if we just stay focused on each other and our process. This is not about one win. This is about being successful on and off the court! Coach Woodward, I once called you a fraud. I was wrong, you are the real deal!" Johnson repeated exactly what Brian Clark said after that game.

"You all have heard the rumors about Coach Woodward's future at Bozeman Tech. You probably read the story online a few weeks ago that said he needed to lead your team to the play-offs and then win the conference championship to keep his job. It was all true because I told him that and then leaked it to the press." Johnson looked at every player who glared back as he paused.

"I learned from you that I needed to look in the mirror, and I did. My own demons from the past affected my judgment and I was dead wrong about Coach Woodward. I have learned from all of you that a culture of WE will defeat the disease of ME every damn time," Johnson stated.

"Today I have two questions, and both are related. Number one, Coach Woodward, can you accept my heartfelt apology and accept me into your culture of WE?" Johnson paused and pulled a paper from his sports jacket pocket, "And two, Coach Woodward, would you please consider this new five-year contract to coach OUR Bison next season and for many seasons to come?"

Woodward walked forward and put his arm around his boss and said, "Alan this is a real family and we believe in personal choice and accountability. We also recognize that we all make mistakes, and we believe our next play is our most important play." Woodward continued, "Gentlemen, Coach Johnson would like to join our team. Do you accept him for who he once was, what he is today, and what he can become?"

"YES, SIR!" was the resounding response.

"OK, we are not done yet. Are you willing to accept me for who I was, what I am today, and what I can become in the future as your head coach now and the years to come?" Woodward asked with passion.

The locker room exploded! Players attacked their coach, poured water on Woodward and Johnson. Coach Geek hugged Coach Woodward and Woodward held him tight and screamed in his ear, "YOU'RE HIRED! YOU WANT A FULL TIME JOB AS AN ASSISTANT?"

Ron Marshall ran out of the locker room and hugged Ellen and Freddy. He told them the great news. Freddy screamed, "Yes! My dad is a real coach!"

As the press gathered just outside the locker room, they heard the raucous noise through the walls, "EVERY DAY IN EVERY WAY WE GET A LITTLE BETTER! EVERY DAY IN EVERY WAY WE GET A LITTLE BETTER! …" They were thinking, *What the heck is going on. This is the team that just lost.*

They were gathered to hear what they thought would be the final words from Coach Woodward, as head coach at Bozeman Tech. Coach Woodward and Alan Johnson came out to face them together.

"Gentlemen, thank you for joining us." Alan Johnson put his arm around Coach Woodward, "Please help me in congratulating Coach Woodward on a tremendous season that included players who earned the best GPA in program history, represented Bozeman Tech with sportsmanship and class, and along the way, won more games than they lost. That last fact, while impressive, was the least important statement I made about their season."

Johnson went on, "I just asked Coach Woodward to continue as our coach for many years to come, and he has graciously accepted our offer to remain the head basketball coach at Bozeman Tech!" Even the media members applauded as Johnson held Woodward's hand in the air.

Woodward was blinded by the camera lights, but he saw Ron, Ellen and Freddy hugging in the background. The media pushed forward with microphones and ESPN cameras focused on the scene where Mark Adams was suddenly standing next to him. Woodward saw Judy and pulled her through the throng next to him and kissed her.

"We are going on SportsCenter with Scott Van Pelt in :15 seconds, Coach Woodward," Adams declared.

"OK," Coach Woodward shot back with a shrug of his shoulders. "Let's do this!"

"Thank you, Scott. I am here with Coach Scott Woodward, the head basketball coach of the Bozeman Tech Bison who just lost their Frontier Conference Championship game in Great Falls. There have been rumors floating about your future as the head coach at Bozeman all week. Coach will you be back to coach Bozeman Tech next season?" Adams asked.

Just then Alan Johnson stepped in, "Mark, all personnel matters go through me, and Scott, if you don't mind, I will answer that question," Johnson moved in. "Coach Woodward has exceeded every expectation both on and off the floor. He has built a culture of success around accountability and the innovative use of technology. More importantly, Coach Woodward has set an example for our entire campus community on how to work through challenges, even when his boss is one of those challenges. I just spoke with Coach Woodward and offered him a long-term contract to continue his great work at Bozeman Tech and he has accepted that offer," Johnson concluded his remarks and stepped away so his coach would now have the ESPN spotlight.

"Coach Woodward, what has it been like working through these challenges at Bozeman Tech when it seemed your job was on the line from day one?" Adams asked.

"It wasn't easy. I had to do some soul searching and I realized my job security or lack thereof was affecting how I managed this team. I had built up a self-centered pressure to win, and I forced it on my players and staff, and that was wrong. I was reminded by some great and loyal friends, and by my own players, that building lifelong relationships and being successful people on and off the court was our goal. And, yes, we incorporated many new and innovative ways to build better accountability across every member of our coaching staff and team. We are a better program today and I am a better person and coach because of that culture shift," Woodward concluded.

"Coach, I'm curious. Can you explain that culture shift and how you used technology to help change your culture?" Adams followed up.

"We decided at Christmas to start over. We attracted a talented technology leader and graduate student here at Bozeman Tech to help us. We have a tremendous technology and leadership program under Dr. Jack Rye," Woodward explained. "That grad student, Ron Marshall, devised a plan with our staff to utilize tech tools for better communication, and better tracking of the right successful behaviors both on and off the court. We figured out how to apply some standard business technologies to monitor our day to day operations. Ron helped us develop a coherent plan to better manage ourselves and our players. We combined ways to leverage the Career Best Efforts from our people first. We did that by developing individual and collective processes for accountability. Then we simply leveraged common business tools to ease the tracking and reporting of our individual and overall team progress."

"Was there a moment when you knew this new way of coaching would work?" Adams asked.

"Yes, Mark. It was after we won our conference opener against Montana A&M. Our halftime adjustments were mostly player-driven because we empowered them and utilized technology to support their goals. We have a unique halftime process where we leverage our video and evaluation tools. We can share important information directly to our players." Woodward continued. "That day, when I walked into our locker room at halftime and saw the players engaged with each other and self-correcting, I knew we were on to something special," Woodward concluded.

"Coach Woodward, earlier this season you were 0-3 and depressed after a 20-point home loss. You told me then you went home that evening and cooked up eighteen pancakes! Why?" Adams asked as Woodward laughed.

"Mark, I was so depressed after that ugly home loss, and I did cook eighteen pancakes. I have no clue as to why, but I gained a few pounds eating all of them!" Woodward laughed.

"Just three months ago Scott Woodward and his team stood at 0-3 and this coach was at home depressed while cooking and eating pancakes. Tonight, this coach and his team stand 16-13 and while they may have lost this one battle, they have built an incredible team foundation and culture for future success! No reason to be depressed over this most improved team in the country." Adams then made one final statement.

"For this coach, THERE WILL BE NO PANCAKES TONIGHT! Scott Van Pelt back you."

Lesson 42

 You never know when your actions and your team's actions will be noticed – maybe even by your boss. Someone is always watching. Your career best effort is an important first step to greater productivity and quality of life. Your life's mission and how you can apply your mission can change your life and the lives of those around you, FOREVER!

THE END

About the Authors

Mark Adams

Lighthouse Technologies, Inc. VP of
Client Success, Judy's husband,
Luke's, Patrick's, Jimmy's and
Robby's Dad, Abby's and Jake's
grandfather, former championship
college basketball coach, and current
national college basketball analyst on
ESPN for over 20 years
www.lighthousetechnologies.com
Connect on LinkedIn
Follow on Twitter

Jeff Van Fleet

Lighthouse Technologies, Inc. CEO,
Sandy's husband, Catie and Rachel's
Dad, Pete & Anna's son, played
trumpet in the Penn State Blue Band,
over 35 years' experience leading
high-performing software and quality
assurance teams
www.lighthousetechnologies.com
Connect on LinkedIn
Follow on Twitter

Notes

Notes

Notes

Notes

Notes

Notes